From Care to Somewhere

Gina Larrisey

authorHOUSE®

AuthorHouse™ UK Ltd.
500 Avebury Boulevard
Central Milton Keynes, MK9 2BE
www.authorhouse.co.uk
Phone: 08001974150

© 2010 Gina Larrisey. All rights reserved.

No part of this book may be reproduced, stored in a retrieval system, or transmitted by any means without the written permission of the author.

First published by AuthorHouse 10/28/2010

ISBN: 978-1-4520-9011-5 (sc)

This book is printed on acid-free paper.

For my husband Shaun who is patient and loves me more than anyone has ever loved anyone.

For Gary who was my rock.

And for my daughter who has her whole life in front of her. May she learn from me and remember always that I love her.

Chapters

Preface	ix
1. Just a Baby	1
2. Rejection	10
3. Home	19
4. Burgled	26
5. Not Again!!	38
6. A Death in the Family	49
7. Young Love	57
8. Another Boyfriend, Another Problem	68
9. The Foster Parents	74
10. Wimbrick Hey	83
11. Parkside (My Home)	87
12. Camp	96
13. Pregnant!	106
14. Not so Sweet Sixteen	110
15. College	120
16. A Fabulous Christmas	126
17. A New Family	134
18. A New Flat	143
19. A Baby Girl	152

20. Damp	160
21. A Serious Accident!	166
22. Three Babies and the To Do List	175
23. Enough is enough	186
24. A Fresh Start	194
25. A Certificate and a Trophy	210
26. The Year 2000	218
27. Eviction	233
28. Ibiza	242
29. I Love You	251
30. The Avon Lady!	260
31. Mysterious Life	270
32. Somewhere	275

Preface

Life is a funny old thing with its ups and downs. Sometimes we struggle through it wondering what it's all about. There are people in far worse situations than I ever was. I wasn't beaten or raped or anything like that. I didn't have the worst childhood either, although it was bad enough to have an effect on me. It was more the mental and emotional rather than physical that screwed my head up.

I was born in 1972 and spent most of my childhood in and out of care. I have been from day centres to foster carers, to children's homes and to hostels. The world hated me so I hated it right back, until a few years ago. I have been in some messes, made many mistakes and somehow I have always managed to come through them. I have been a single parent, and lived with anti social behaviour. I have been unemployed and divorced twice.

Maybe my eagerness to please people is what has led me to take on so many challenges, and I have worked very hard to achieve my goals.

This is my story of how I got, "From Care to Somewhere".

1. Just a Baby

It was the 24th November in 1972, just a month before Christmas. A five month old baby was taken in to care. It was supposed to be a temporary measure. The baby's mother had confided in a social worker that she had hit the baby a few times and was scared she may do so again. That baby was me. I was born in June of the same year and little did I know at the tender age of only five months that this temporary measure would turn out to be just the start of my life in and out of care.

I was placed at Prenton Dell Reception Centre in Birkenhead, where according to them I appeared to settle well. From there, five days later, I was placed into the care of Foster Parents. I actually had no idea about this until I applied for and received my file from the Social Services a few years ago. My Mum still to this day has never ever mentioned it.

A social worker visited me on the 30th November to lend the lady I was staying with a pram. She noted that I was sleeping well, eating well and looked contented. A day later Mum was asking to see me. She was in fact in hospital at this time suffering with depression. The sister on the ward agreed with the social worker that it would be a good thing if I was taken to see her there.

A few days later I was taken to the hospital to visit

Mum. Visiting Mum in the hospital was to become a regular thing as she suffered from manic depression and would be admitted periodically. Mum was pleased that I looked so well and she sat me on her knee. I smiled and gurgled at her contentedly. She received as much information as possible about my routine and about the fact that I had had a rash from a woollen shawl I had been wearing the day before. She apparently looked much better and was hoping to be back home for Christmas. My Dad was at home apparently coping better than had been expected in their high-rise flat on the seventh floor whilst Mum was in the hospital. They were planning to move but, not having much joy with the housing situation they decided to think about buying a place of their own. When I began to get restless Mum handed me back to the social worker and I was taken back to the Foster Parents.

A month later I was discharged from care and went back home to Mum and Dad in time for Christmas. Frequent visits were then made by the social worker. Then in March 1973, when I was nine months old I was taken to a clinic where Mum stated she had come to hand me over and she was going to run away. It was urged for us to be re-housed. Mum became resentful of me because of this and it was felt that I may be *at risk* because of her depression and their occupation of a high-rise flat. We were re-housed to a two bedroom low-rise flat in 1974.

I was seen that same year at a luncheon club that Mum was helping out at. It is reported that I was clean, well dressed and well fed.

My baby sister was born in July 1974. Now there were two of us to worry about.

Then just over a year later the cycle recommenced. In November 1975 when I was just three and my sister was only 16 months old, a health visitor made a telephone call to the social worker extremely concerned for my well being. It would appear that my Mum had no maternal feelings for me at all and my Dad was both inadequate and rejecting. Mum was afraid that she might harm me. There were no signs of physical ill treatment, though it appeared there were more behavioural signs. I had become very attention seeking, unable to relate, quiet and more withdrawn. I was regressing.

A few days later there was another telephone call to the social worker from the day nursery that I was now attending. It seemed that my Dad had gone there at 5 pm. He said he was going back home and then coming back to collect me from the nursery. *At 5 pm?* The nursery worker pointed out to my Dad that the nursery would then be closed. He told her to close up as usual and to leave me alone in the garden. *What was he thinking?*

He also stated that he was removing me from the nursery as it was far too expensive. The nursery also reported that I had regressed and was not talking as much.

In light of all this the social worker then made a visit to us in early December. Mum seemed very depressed (something that my sister and I would have to get used to). Mum and Dad were facing eviction in the New Year. Dad was unemployed with very little money so it was no wonder they couldn't afford the bus fares to the nursery. The social worker aired her concerns for me and Mum admitted to being less patient with me and putting me in my room by myself for long periods of time. Both my sister and I were said to be well dressed. The social worker offered help by asking the nursery if they would consider a free placement for me and then the bus fares to and from were to be organised by the Social Services department.

Following this more telephone calls were made out of concern for me. It was felt that my personality was changing. I was taken out of the nursery which was then reported to Social Services, and so the social worker then visited our flat. Mum answered the door in her nightdress, she looked thin, pale and, *'out of this world'*. She could give no reason as to why I was not at the day nursery and she was very worried about her financial situation. My sister and I were in the bedroom. The social worker asked to see us so my Dad came and fetched us from the bedroom. I had dressed myself and my sister was still in her nighty. She was blue with the cold. Apparently although it was almost dinner time this was just normality and neither of us had eaten since the previous evening. Dad was very excitable, irrational and full of daft ideas as to how to solve their financial difficulties. The social worker pointed out that eighteen hours was a long time for us to go without food. My Dads reply to this was: *"They'll have to tighten their belts the same as us."*

I know that my Dad was one of six boys who grew up in Liverpool. There is not much else I do know about him. He too grew up in care though and I know that my Mum lost her Mum at a young age and had a rough childhood. Maybe they just didn't have a clue how to bring us up in view of their own childhoods. They were both victims of circumstance too.

The concerned social worker tried to organise a meeting regarding our welfare. We were again visited by the social worker a few days later with another social worker (Mrs Gee) in tow. My Dad answered the door obviously in an angry mood. Mum too was most unwelcoming in her attitude and both were indignant that we were considered to be in any way neglected. Mum calmed down. To be fair my Mum isn't the confrontational type. My Dad seemed to lose the plot though exhibiting his volatile nature, shouting and thumping the coffee table. I think I must get my temper from him. He did eventually calm down. It was pointed out to Mum and Dad that we did require three meals a day and should not go so long without food. Mum told the social worker that my Dad was getting her down as he was at home for part of the day due to not working. When he was actually at home I don't know because according to the social worker it was noted that he had done about 7000 miles on his motor bike in the previous six months. Mum asked if the social worker would visit again and would welcome some clothes for us. **Hang on!** My Dads running a motor bike and we need clothes?! *Well I can see why he was doing my mums head in!!*

The spring of my third year approached. I was now attending Cavendish Day Nursery, largely due to my father's overt rejection of me. He had hit me and used the stereo to toilet train me by shouting down the microphone at me: "**Gina you must go to the toilet, Gina you must go to the toilet!**" I always remember being scared of the loud speakers and microphone.

Unfortunately it was decided that I was to be taken out of this nursery too as it was too much trouble for

Mum to pick me up in the evenings. She had written a note saying so and also that Dad had got a job at Triumph, in Speke.

One afternoon in March 1976 Mum telephoned Social Services asking for a visit from them which they did. She wanted me to go to Vyner Primary School and had already been and spoken to the headmaster. She said that she was phobic about travelling on buses with us but the social worker doubted how true this was, as it had not been mentioned before. The social worker also stated that I was at home when she called and in her words: *'It was quite apparent the mother is irritated by the child.'*

Mum asked the social worker if it was possible to move things a long a little quicker with regards as to getting me in to the school. At this point my Dad came in, very belligerent and aggressive although he later apologised for this. The report doesn't say why he was so angry. It was later agreed with the school that they could take me for a half day.

A month later Mum rang the office again asking if Tracey (my sister) and I could be placed into care as she was due for an operation on one of her legs in early May. She insisted our Dad couldn't have cared for us as he was incapable. It was decided that we would go to Foster Parents in Wallasey. In the mean time Dad intended to sell the motorbike and the debts they had were slowly being paid off. Mum was quite pleased about that.

Tracey and I were both picked up at the end of April and taken to our new home. Mum was very concerned for my little sister. Her concerns for me that day were over the fact that I had marked our bedroom wall with the end of a sweeping brush. Mum and Dad had been really angry over it. Funny!! I remember actually doing this too. It gave me great pleasure bashing the wall with the end of the brush and I remember liking the shapes it made in the plaster. I hadn't realized I had done anything wrong at the time. Well I was only three!

A few days later Tracey was fretting for Mum. I had settled in ok. I remember our first night there. It was so strange as the bedroom had the very same curtains and bedding as we had at home. I lay there trying to figure it out. As it turned out it <u>was</u> our bedding and curtains. Somebody thought it was a great idea for us to have familiar objects around us. It just confused the hell out of me!

My foster mother, Mrs Leton, said she found me to be over anxious and eager to please. I don't really remember her at all. One day I had had an accident in my pants and her words were that I was *'terrified'*. This wasn't the first time I was terrified after having an accident. I remember at home the flat being full of people and desperately trying to get past peoples legs to the toilet. There must have been some kind of party. I didn't make it. I was distraught. Mum reassured me it was ok and put me in the bath. I was to find out why I was terrified after reading on in my file and how id been potty trained over the stereo

On the 10th of May Mum telephoned the department again asking if we could stay with Mr and Mrs Leton for longer. This was discussed with Mrs Gee and it was decided that no, we were to go home. At the entrance to our flat I did not want to go in. Mums attitude towards me was unwelcoming. The file said there were no *'affectionate overtones'* towards myself but she took Tracey straight on to her knee. She said that Dad was ill in bed (he also suffered with a mental disorder according to my file), her legs were painful and she didn't know how she would cope.

A week later, on another visit Mum told the social worker she had hit me and given me a nose bleed. She had lost her temper with me. I have four children of my own now so I know how stressful it can be sometimes. Sometimes people do lash out without thinking. The school were asked to keep an eye out for me and to make sure I got a good meal at school as money was tight at home.

With autumn upon us, it was around this time that I recall being taken for a walk. The crisp autumn leaves in all their bright colours stick out vividly in my mind. Tracey was in her pram and I was walking alongside. For some reason Dad always refused to let me hold Mums hand. This was a regular thing. He said I was too old. *At four years of age?* I was most upset and cried the whole time. Dad made me stay at the bottom of what appeared to be quite a big hill to me (I was only little so it probably looked bigger than it actually was). He told me I had to stay there and a big bad wolf would get me if I didn't stop crying.

In October 1976 we were yet again to be carted off. A different foster parent this time, a lady called, Mrs Ray. On reception in to care I was found to have a four inch diagonal bruise at the bottom of my spine. I said my Dad had smacked me hard with a slipper because I had been naughty. Mum was said to have felt like knifing him when he hit us. She was in hospital again with depression and feeling very weepy. The family problems had escalated to a deplorable state. Mum had said she was torn between her children and our Dad. She felt that he must take priority as she considered him her third child. We had been kept in our rooms away from him to safeguard us. We were kept quiet as he could not stand us chattering on and he had also apparently hit us on several occasions. In her depressed state she repeated that *'the only way out was to overdose us and take one herself'*. We were taken to see her in hospital but we were both uneasy and evidently upset by our surroundings so the visit was kept short.

Action would now be taken for our parents' rights to be removed as Tracey and I were both showing signs of acutely disturbed behaviour.

2. Rejection

Our stay at, the Rays' would last for six weeks in all. Here I displayed more signs of behavioural problems. Well was it any wonder with all this to-ing and fro-ing? At school the signs were so apparent that the Foster Parents met up with the school to discuss the matter. They reported *'Gina is disruptive and rude'* but that there had been an improvement. No improvement with my parents though, unfortunately. There were increasing signs of mental deterioration, our needs were not being met and there was no doubt that our development was being impaired. There seemed to be no alternative for Social Services but to take action to safeguard us. It was reported: *'The children have suffered and continue to do so.'* Both our parents had psychiatrists who strongly backed up Social Services with regards to removing their rights to care for us.

Through October, Mum made several phone calls. She was missing us and wanted to see us. We had a few visits but they were kept short. Mum was discharged home on 19th November. We were returned to our parents' care ten days later, against the advice of the Social Services department. The social worker took us home in the afternoon and said that Mum only welcomed us home briefly before plunging into details of her finances. Dad had been overspending on the motorbike and sidecar. Evidently he had decided not to sell it after all and Mum had thought it was a good idea for getting out on day trips and things. I can see where she was coming from. She probably thought it would help by doing things together as a family. I remember sitting in the sidecar on a purple cushion and Tracey would be sat on mums knee. We had gone out on the bike one evening to get lights for the Christmas tree. Funny how it always seemed to be just before Christmas that we would go back home!

Just a few days before Christmas, the social worker visited us again. Mum was very upset as she had only been able to buy Tracey a present but not me. The social worker wrote that this was *'significant as Gina is the rejected child'*. She came back the next day with a hamper and some presents that had been donated to the office. Mum was made up as she received a tea set which she decided to give me. I loved playing with the bright red tea set I received. I hid behind the chest of drawers in my bedroom and spat in the cups. **Eeeeeee!!!!** I was pretending that it was real tea until my Dad caught me doing it. He was so tall that he towered over the unit and caught me peeping up from behind my little red tea cup. From what I do remember of the Christmases I did spend at home, we always got loads of presents and had a good time. Mum did do her best for us in that department.

With Christmas behind us the family problems escalated again. Mum was said to have felt like taking too many tablets and had been to see the doctor regarding this. Dad had received some money that he'd been owed and decided to pay some outstanding bills. He was busy knitting jumpers. Mum always said that he was a clever man.

Rejection

In March 1977 Mum was once again admitted to hospital suffering with severe depression. My sister and I were again placed in to care under section 1 of the Children and Young Persons Act 1948, whatever that is! We were homed with, Mr and Mrs Leton again.

During our stay we both got chicken pox. I was apparently very ill with it. I was also found to be very chesty and had to have wheezing tablets for my asthma. I remember quite clearly when we had the chickenpox. We had to both stand outstretched and very still whilst we were dabbed all over with calamine lotion. Any visits to Mum would not be possible now. Our stay this time would be a longer one. I now went to St George's primary school in Wallasey. I was said to settle down well, was bright and alert. I walked to the school with my foster sister through a graveyard.

I remember one day being made to walk through on my own. I wasn't scared of the graveyard, just scared of being left alone. I checked around me as I hurried through to the other side. At Easter I made an egg basket in class and carried it carefully out to my Foster Parents when they picked me up at home time. I remember looking up at the sash windows of the school on my way out of the school gates. I don't remember much else of them really, I was still very young. Just silly things like the bowls we had our cereal in. Ginger bread men we'd had one evening after a chippy tea and a time when I'd fallen over and scraped my knee.

In April our parents were visited by the social worker. Mum was supposed to be in the hospital but instead was flapping over Dad and had been released for the day. On her arrival she noticed how ill Dad looked: *'Thin and emaciated as always,'* as the description in my file said. Whilst she was present, an incident occurred outside the flat. Someone had shot an air gun at our living room window, cracking it. Dad went off his head shouting and yelling, which I personally think was understandable! He then jumped up thumping the glass out of it. Glass was flying everywhere. He cut himself in doing this so an ambulance was called, as the cut seemed quite bad. It was thought he may need stitches. Mum tried to calm him down with a cup of tea. Well, a good old brew can work wonders for me!

Mum went into the Social Services office a few days later with a view to having us back home. She was advised it was not a good idea as she had only recently been discharged from hospital.

On the 11th May, a month before my fifth birthday, arrangements were made for Tracey and me to visit Mum and Dad at the office late in the afternoon. Mum was evidently very happy to see Tracey but I was said to be rather left out. Dad was attentive to neither of us. Two weeks on and our parents were said to be seeking advice from solicitors with regards to having us both back home. It seems that there was conflict with various parties such as doctors and health visitors over the matter and a case conference was decided upon to discuss our welfare.

The case conference was held on the 17th June 1977. That same day we were taken to see our parents at the office again. It reads in my file:

'The pattern of reception and interaction continues. The children run to their mother who always turns to Tracey

first and picks her up. After the initial greeting Tracey receives more attention and Gina is largely ignored. She often asks questions which are parentally not heard and left unanswered. Eventually the children tend to conclude the interview by asking if their parents are going'.

We were returned home to the Foster Parents.

On another occasion, on the way to the office I chatted away to the social worker and asked a lot of questions. At least *she* thought I was, *'a bright little girl'*. I talked about Mum and Dad and reiterated that daddy's hand was big and he smacked hard. I sought reassurance from her and often tested out. At the office Mum did make an effort to prove she was capable of having us back home but I think it was probably too late by then. She knew she could fight to get us back home but it was thought that perhaps she wouldn't. The social worker liked my Mum but felt she had to put our needs first. Parental rights were assumed on the 6th July 1977.

It turns out that Mum did fight to get us back home. She constantly telephoned the Social Services department and attempted to organise meetings. It was explained to her over and over again why and how the steps had been taken to keep us in care. Dad flipped his lid and threatened to go to the local newspapers. Mum sought advice and support elsewhere but oddly mentioned that she was thinking of having another baby. WHAT??? She couldn't have been thinking straight.

In September another visit to the office was to be significant. I had brought a teddy bear in with me and my Dad thought it would be funny to tease me by constantly taking it off me and then giving it me back. He took great pleasure in watching my upset at this and repeated his mean trick over and over again. Mum and the social worker kept on at him to stop but he carried on until he had reduced me and my Mum to tears. Why did she put up with this? She must have loved him that's all I'm saying. I sat on the social workers knee and cried quite obviously upset. Dad knew what he was doing was cruel and Mum was not happy with him.

This was not the only time Dad displayed cruelty towards me. On or around one bonfire night I was quite disturbed by the noise of the fireworks. I had my tea in front of me of toast, egg, cheese and beans. *Urrgghh!!* I didn't want to eat it but Dad said if I didn't get it ate he would put my bare bum out of the window and the fireworks would hit it, quite frightening to a four year old.

He was very dominating and towered above me at another time belting out *Chanson D'Amour* over his microphone and, *Rat a Tat a Tat*. I remained fixed to the black leather settee we had and I fell asleep. When I woke I was fascinated at how the green fruit polo I had been sucking had shrunk in my mouth…

October saw us with a change of social worker. I have very fond memories of Mr Dennis. He used to take us to the office for our visits and I loved him so much I christened him Dad. Our visits to the office on Cleveland Street in Birkenhead were very enjoyable.

Through October and November over several visits with our parents, Mum discussed at great length the possibility of having us returned home to her. I don't doubt that Mum and Dad had a rough time. The situation must have caused problems in their marriage as separation and divorce were mentioned and our being in care was, according to them, to blame. However, the situation was accepted for the time being and a lot of effort was made in a bid to sort out their difficulties. They visited us once a fortnight. Dad was trying to get a job and had interviews lined up as a driver. It wasn't too long before things went wrong again though as in early December my parents finally agreed to separate. Not only were our parents about to start divorce proceedings but we were about to be moved for the umpteenth time to different Foster Parents too. Unfortunately the, Letons were not interested in long term fostering so it seemed we were to be moved on again.

On the 10th December we were transferred to new Foster Parents in Bebington. We would be with this family for five months. I was now five and a half and my sister was three. I remember being taken to our new family. I was given some paper and crayons to colour a picture on my arrival. I remember being fascinated by the water print on my sheet of paper and tried to colour it in.

At Christmas Mum must have had some Christmas presents sent on for us as I remember the doll I received. I've never seen a doll so big in all my life. It was as big as me and frightened the living daylights out of me. I hated it!! I don't remember much else of these Foster Parents either, only the little things, like the Foster Dad used to wear a big boot because he had one leg shorter than the other and one time when I sat playing with a doll on the grass in the back garden. I could hear Tracey crying from upstairs in the bathroom. I was worried about her as she didn't like the water going over her face when being bathed. I was sure they were tipping it over her and making her scream.

Our father was to walk out of our lives for good at this point, only visiting the Social Services office once in a bid to gain access but was sadly refused and told to stay away. *Why did we not have supervised access?* After all is said and done he was still our Dad.

Mums visits began to be more regular after Christmas. The little church on the estate where we lived agreed for us to have supervised access there with some of the church members. This was the support that my Mum had sought out. These visits were very successful. Mum made a lot of friends at the chapel and we all have fond memories of it.

With my change of Foster Parents came another change of school. This time it was Brackenwood Junior School. Tracey was now at an age where she could attend nursery. Her speech was said to have improved dramatically following our arrival at our new Foster Parents.

By March our once a week visits were increased to twice a week. It seems that things had improved since Dads departure.

By April things were looking up and weekends at home were arranged. When it was time to go back to the Foster Parents after our weekends at home we didn't want to leave Mum. Mrs Gee would have to assist our departure as we were so distraught. In light of the fact that Mum was adamant her divorce was going ahead, and as Dad was no longer on the scene, the decision was made to allow us back home again permanently. Our return to our rightful place with our Mum was to take place on May 19th 1978. However, the authorities would retain the parental rights.

3. Home

It was Friday 19th May 1978. We did indeed return to our mothers care and went home to our flat on the Ford Estate. I remember a photographer coming to take our picture outside the flat for the local newspaper as it was such a happy occasion. Mum had fought to get us back home and that was the story. Tracey and I were dressed in matching outfits (which we often were) of little denim blue skirts with white lace on the pockets and white frilly tops. I was clutching my rabbit teddy. People often commented about us and asked "Are they twins?" because of our similar cute looks with our blonde hair and blue eyes.

On our arrival home Mum said we were to be very quiet as she had a surprise for us in the kitchen. We tiptoed in to find a tiny tortoiseshell kitten hiding under the kitchen table. A new family member called Kitty to love.

I turned six in June a month later. Once again our return was not without problems as Mums depression was not going to go away. Every little minor crisis fuelled her depression even more. Visits were made by, Mr Dennis virtually on a day to day basis. A home-maker (as they were called then) was employed to help out but even she found Mums depression hard to handle. A notice to quit had been received from the housing department in the following July but with support from Mr Dennis the problem was dealt with. Mr Dennis wrote that if things revert back to the way they were he envisaged a fostering situation once more.

I still continued to have temper tantrums, mainly at school. Ballantyne Infants was my third school now and I remember the screaming fits I used to have all too often. By now my head was well messed up and the frustration inside me used to just explode. One day I was made to sit on the teacher's knee during one of these screaming fits. I had thrown a paddy because I didn't want to sing *Oh-bla-Dee, Oh bla-Dah life goes on.* I thought it was a swear word and that I would get into trouble. Mum told me that when she had picked me up at home time she could hear my tantrum from outside by the school gates. I remember feeling embarrassed. She complained of these tantrums to Mr Dennis. I refused to go to school on occasions and Mum was told to be firm with me.

Another tantrum I'd had at home resulted in me saying I was running away. I promptly packed all my toys and belongings in my purple padded dressing gown and ran out of the front door shouting "I hate you, I hate you." Mum shouted back to me "I hate you too," and she shut the door. Not what I wanted to hear. I just needed reassurance that she loved me. Tracey had been affected in a different way to me. I was the one with all the anger on the surface, always ready to explode but Tracey kept all hers in. She just shut herself off from the world. This impaired her progress so much so she eventually needed to go to a school for Special Needs children to help her to catch up.

A few different home-makers started to come on a

regular basis now. They were all like aunties to us and we loved them all. We got so excited when they came to see us. Things settled down by September and Social Services then considered backing off. Mum was most upset at this. Her impending divorce hearing meant that support would be necessary for a while longer. The divorce was granted in November 1978, almost a year after proceedings had started. This must have been a very sad time for her. Although Mum and Dad were not good together, that doesn't stop you loving someone and feeling emotional when it's over.

Six months passed and all was well. No sign of Dad now for a long time, which made Mum's life easier. She was hoping to be re-housed somewhere with a garden for us to play in.

In the meantime, a party was held at the flat for my seventh birthday. A huge white blanket was laid out on the living room floor (or maybe it was lots of small ones) and food was put out for everyone. There were cakes and jellies. Mum was a cracking cook and no doubt she made the butterfly cakes herself. She would cut a round out of the top of the cake and cut that in half for the wings, fill the hole with butter cream and place the wings on top. Tracey and I always looked forward to "bake day" when we got to lick the spoon after cake mixture had been made. Loads of people came to the party which was a great success. I remember receiving pink rosebud bobbles, pink and white checked ribbons for my hair and a wildlife book amongst other things.

In the summer Mum would take us for picnics to Thermopylae pass at Bidston Hill. She would take a blanket to sit on and a picnic of egg sandwiches. I always wondered why she wrapped them in a damp tea towel. She said it was to keep them fresh. We would have a bottle of cherryade which was a real treat. The fizziness spat in your face as you attempted to drink it. Tracey and I would roly-poly down the hills there and we would go for walks past the big posh houses in Bidston. Mum loved the bright pink rhododendrons in full bloom on the walks and we would always think wishfully about which house we were going to live in one day.

In early August Mum's patience in the house hunting department was rewarded. A three bedroom house with a little garden not too far from the flat became vacant. The chapel that had supported Mum throughout her efforts to have us returned home the previous year was a stone's throw away too, which was good news. Tracey and I were to share a bedroom. It had flowery wallpaper and our same matching bedding and curtains were hung up. The beds sat side by side. The spare bedroom was made into a toy room for us to play in. I spent many a rainy day here colouring away quite contentedly. In fact I was very artistic which did come to Mum's notice.

Eleven months passed with just monthly visits from Mr Dennis. The home-makers remained as part of our weekly routine and during this time life was somewhat normal. My sister and I played together and fought together. We listened to Cliff Richard records and Mum's soppy albums of love songs. We attended the chapel on a weekly basis and we played in the woods which were right next to our house. Kitty, our cat chased and killed a little mouse one day and so we buried it in these woods. We gave the tiny creature a proper burial and said prayers for it. Mum had a garden to attend to now and in this she realised a new found interest. She would be out there for hours weeding and digging her rockery. She would tell me all the names of the plants and shrubs. This must be where I get my love for gardening from. Very therapeutic! On my eighth birthday she made me a gorgeous fresh strawberries and cream birthday cake. She said it was special birthday sponge. To this day it is the most delicious cake I've ever tasted. Life was quite good for a short while.

Our great granddad was of good support to Mum too. He often would send money to Mum to help her out. He lived in a tiny one bed roomed cottage in Chirk (Wales) with his third wife. I can still smell the tomatoes he grew in his back garden. The cottage was situated on a tiny picturesque bridge that stretched over a canal. The odd summer was spent here together. It was a holiday to us and a much needed break away for Mum. After our long journey on the train to Wales we would always have a colouring book full of butterflies and a packet of coloured pencils waiting for us on our arrival. We would all three of us sleep in Granddads bed, Mum in the middle and us either side of her (so Tracey and I couldn't fight). Granddad couldn't manage the stairs any more and had a bed in the living room. In the morning I would wake up to the most glorious sunshine streaming through the gaps in the curtains. The whole bedroom was orange aglow and warm with the morning sunshine. We would go for long walks in the countryside and along the aqueduct, where butterflies in all their radiant colour were plentiful. The smell of the nearby chocolate factory was subject to many discussions and Mum would browse for ages around the Welsh craft shops after taking us to the swings in the park. We were happy here.

Mum's depression and mental state got the better of her again in early July. I must have noticed as I had commented that she had started smoking again. The report said she had *'regressed to a very serious degree and [was] displaying all the signs of the deep depression of earlier times'*. She had been to the doctor and was taking medication to combat this. Being aware that hospital admission was likely, she knew we would probably be taken in to care again. Knowing how previously our times in and out of care had badly damaged us she did not want us to go through any more upheaval than was necessary. Steps were taken to have us admitted to care but unbeknown to the Social Services department Mum had made her own plans. She was petrified of losing us for good and refused to tell Mr Dennis where we were staying. She believed that if he were to find out we would be taken forever and moved to somewhere where she could not find us. She arranged for us to stay with our aunty and uncle in Preston for a week. We were told we were going away for a little holiday and that is what I recall of it, unaware that Mum was ill again. I am assuming our stay at our uncle and auntie's house was very brief as no more details have been given.

Four months on and it was felt that the home-makers were no longer required so they were withdrawn. Mum was assured that if any assistance were needed, Mr Dennis was only a phone call away. She had kept a part time cleaning job for a while now and was coping much better with every day life. Both Tracey and I were boisterous and excitable children but considered to be completely normal.

In particular I was quite demanding and attention seeking but Mum was said to over react to my demanding ways most of the time. What child isn't demanding? I would say I had good reason to be!

In February 1981 I was referred to a child psychiatrist from the child and family therapy unit. We were seen at the centre shortly afterwards at Mum's request. In the psychiatrist's opinion there did not appear to be anything abnormal in my behaviour. We were just lively kids. His advice was that we needed help and support in getting along as a family and that my life should not be affected by my Mums life. The sad fact is that this is exactly what did happen. My attention seeking ways were my way of "testing out" and I still needed reassurance that I was loved.

A few months later brought a disaster of another kind.

4. Burgled

In the early hours one morning I was woken by Mum sobbing and whispering to me to wake up. She was quiet so as not to wake Tracey. Quite startled at this hour in the morning, I rubbed the sleep from my eyes wondering why I was being woken in the middle of the night and was shocked to discover from Mum that we had been burgled. Not only that but we had been burgled by the next door neighbours while we were in our beds. I couldn't believe it. I had slept through the whole thing! Poor Mum! Talk about bad luck.

I was honoured that she felt the need to tell someone and that someone was me. She proceeded to tell me how the neighbours had got in through the small back kitchen window and opened the back door. They had acted like a human conveyer belt passing our belongings out and down the line, over the fence and in to next door. As luck would have it someone in the high-rise flats over the road must have been looking out of their window and witnessed the whole thing. They had phoned the police and our house had become subject to the scene of an armed raid and the thieves were caught red handed. Mum didn't have a clue what had happened until the police knocked on the door waking her up with the bad news. They had taken the record player and records and other valuables. The neighbours were arrested and we got all our belongings back. Well almost all. Going in to the fridge for milk the next day I commented on how empty the fridge was. On checking the freezer and fridge Mum realized that they had even taken half tubs of margarine and joints of meat. What a bunch of sado's!

This unfortunate event sent Mum on a downward spiral again making her ill. Well you wouldn't want to live next door to someone that tried to rob you blind would you? She panicked at what might have happened had she heard them that night and gone to look. As a result of the nasty shock she'd had, another spell in hospital was the outcome. The homemakers were sent in to care for us again (much to our delight) so that we wouldn't have to be fostered out again. We could stay in our own home until Mum was well enough to come back. We missed her and occupied ourselves making a huge welcome home poster with glitter and stickers for her on her return. For the next few weeks Mum intensified her efforts along with Mr Dennis and the Social Services department to move from the estate we were living on once and for all. She had good grounds now for a move.

"I'm having this room!" I shouted excitedly banging around on the floor boards. I stomped across the bare wood to the window and looked out at the garden below. It was a dream house. I was to have a room of my own when we moved. There wasn't even a roof on the house we'd come to look at. The houses were brand new, just being built on a brand new estate and had huge front and rear gardens. Maybe being burgled was a blessing in disguise! We had been offered this house and Mum jumped at the chance. This was a new start for all of us in a lovely new area. Mum had grown up as a child around the corner and her Dad (our other Granddad) lived nearby.

We moved to our new home on 12th June 1981, the day before my ninth birthday. Tracey and I were picked up from school and taken to, not the house with no roof that we had ran around so excitedly, but the one next door to it. I watched out of the car window on our journey there wanting to shout to everyone, "Yeah, we're moving!"

The only thing I would really miss was Joanne, my best and only friend since I was seven. I had been a loner at school and she was a bit different like me because she didn't have any of her baby teeth. We had been inseparable, often getting in to trouble for laughing uncontrollably in class. I wrote her a letter at my new home telling her I missed her and made a paper aeroplane out of it. I threw it out of my bedroom window believing that it would somehow reach her. I cried as it sunk to the ground in the rain along with my heart.

Another new home meant another new school, this time Green bank Junior School. Here I settled well and there were no problems to speak of. My teacher, Miss Evans was particularly fond of me. I was very artistic and creative in writing stories and was keen to impress. One afternoon, in a history lesson about the Tudors and the Stuarts, we were designing front covers for our files. I had made a large red Tudor rose to stick on the front. I coated my Tudor rose with glue as when the glue dries it goes shiny. Everyone knows that! I wanted my rose to be shiny. A boy in my class who lived in our road saw what I was doing and being a proper horror himself tried to get me in to trouble by telling Miss what I'd done. Miss told me off and smacked my hand completely at a loss as to why I would be gluing the top of my rose. I cried with disappointment. She then gave me the opportunity to explain, so I did.

She told me "Woe betide if that rose doesn't shine."

But of course it did and I then received two gold stars for my efforts which pleased me immensely. That wiped the grin off my classmate's face!

Another time Miss Evans organised a class competition. She had set aside three ornaments, a mummy frog and two matching baby frogs. The three best stories to be written would each receive one of these cute creatures to take home. It had to be a six chapter story about our chosen subject. I set about my story with gallons of enthusiasm. I got my inspiration from a comic I'd recently read and adapted it with my own imagination. It was complete with a magic gate and woodland animals with jewelled eyes. Miss Evans was so impressed that I won hands down. My six part story was read out to the class who listened quietly. I took all three frogs home that day to treasure. I was very proud and to this day one of the baby frogs still sits on my mantelpiece. The reason I only have one left is another story…

I relished Miss Evans attention and was sad when she retired. Mum encouraged me to make her a leaving card and provided me with sequins and glue. I created a master piece and proudly presented it to my teacher on the last day of term. She was thrilled and said it would have pride of place on her bedside cabinet.

The head teacher and my new class teacher didn't have

any complaints about my behaviour either. My tantrums only ever took place at home now. In fact he commented at one of the case reviews (which were held every six months) how I was happy to join in and that I was a talented artist.

I had drawn and beautifully coloured a picture of a brooch for a story being told in our class for assembly one day. It was my job to stand up and hold it up high so everybody could see it clearly as the story was being told. I was very proud. The school choir was another of my interests. I remember performing for Joseph and his Technicolor dream coat. All those colours, the red and yellow and ochre and…

At Christmas I was in the production of He's Only a Baby. The entire choir wore red gowns and we sang the carols with enthusiasm to accompany the nativity play. The gowns were quite stifling with big white ruffs around the neck. Very antwacky! The girl standing next to me had left all her clothes on underneath her gown and promptly fainted as she overheated in the middle of our performance. As we were at the back standing on benches at the time she had to be rescued by the headmaster. He leapt up very dramatically nearly knocking me over in the process. I remained steadfast singing away doing my best to be professional.

I had been in a nativity play once before at infants school (I'm not sure which one) when I was about four or five. The names were being called out in class for who was playing which part and I had been chosen to play an angel. I couldn't believe it when the teacher called out my name. ME! I had been given the part of an angel. I was made up. My blonde hair and blue eyes must have made me the right choice. I felt as if I had never been noticed before but obviously I had. I wore my white gown and huge feathered wings and donned tinsel on a lifted wire around my head as a halo. I slowly walked out on to the stage on cue to the choir singing the line "Angels bending near the earth, to touch their harps of gold" from It Came Upon the Midnight Clear. I scanned the room looking for Mum. I think she was there but I just couldn't see her and desperately wanted her to be proud of me.

On 27th January 1982, Mum was delighted to learn that she now had her full parental rights again. They remained in place, as did the arrangement with regard to Dad: this was a relief to her.

March brought us another new social worker – Mrs Beech took over from Mr Dennis. She visited by way of an introduction and found Tracey and I to be very lively! At a previous meeting it had been suggested that my sister might attend a movement and dance group. It was thought it would be of benefit to her. Mum said it would cause trouble if I didn't also go and so arrangements were made for both of us to attend. Well I quite agree, you can't give one without the other as I have found out with my own children!

We were introduced to the lady who ran the dance group and we showed off, making conversation difficult between her and Mum. Mum was never very firm with us and we took advantage of that. The dance group started in July and although the teacher reported that we were fine and there were *'no problems away from the mother'*, she said that I was not quite relaxed. Relaxed? I **hated** it. I felt like a right pleb!!

At the end of July, Mum telephoned the office to speak to Mrs Beech but she was away on holiday. It was two weeks later before a visit was finally made. The visit that Mum had requested was due to her overreaction to an incident involving me and a neighbour's child. To be honest I can't even remember it. It must have been a stupid kiddie thing that had been totally blown out of proportion and a week later it's all yesterday's pizza!

Apparently, I had become hysterical when one of my friends had fallen out with me and told everyone else not to play with me any more. Mrs Beech explained to her that this kind of reaction was normal in any child who had a history such as mine being in and out of care for years. Mum said it was a relief that I'd been fine in getting over the quarrel. I don't understand! Where was the problem then? Why was the visit still necessary two weeks later? My immature and emotional state and my approaching puberty were discussed.

Every now and then, Mum would let me stay up a little later than Tracey at bedtimes so that we might have that extra one-to-one together. She cuddled me and told me she loved me but that I couldn't behave the way I was. At ten years old now my head was full of confusion. She said one thing to me but often her actions spoke differently. My age may have been partly the reason for my outbursts but mainly it was due to my past and feelings of rejection. Mrs Beech said that I did appear to be a perfectionist, always wanting to be the best and Mum agreed, saying I must have inherited this from Dad, as he was never happy with second best either. The reality is I felt that if I wasn't perfect I would be rejected again, thus my eagerness to please constantly. Mrs Beech left with the knowledge that Mum was expecting more trouble from me.

Summer had arrived and the school holiday was now in full swing. Trips and picnics had been on the agenda but somehow they just didn't happen. Mum had hoped that her Dad would take us all out to Chester Zoo but as he hadn't offered we didn't go. Tracey and I were wild with energy. We had a paddling pool in the back garden and a Wendy house but we never quite got on together anymore. We fought when playing Barbie weddings both insisting our Barbie doll was going to be the princess. It would always end up in a fight. The overall tension had affected our relationship. We argued a lot and Mum said our 'love-hate' relationship was stronger than normal.

Mum had tried giving me a corner of the garden the year before to occupy me but the novelty soon wore off. At first I grew marigolds and made a rockery like the one at our old house but I tired of it when the weeds started to come up. When we had first moved here the whole garden was the remains of the builders' site and it was full of bricks. Before the houses were built the land had been a pig farm so Mum kept finding bones in the soil. She had dug it all over and I had hoed it. She made rockery's again like at our last house and our Granddad put up a trellis for a climbing rose to ramble up. She made it beautiful. I did enjoy helping her out in the garden and she rewarded me with some pocket money for my efforts. I knew exactly what I was going to buy. I loved to collect ornaments and had seen a beautiful glass wishing well with a tiny bird on it. I treasured it on a shelf in my bedroom. My prize for a job well done! That was until Tracey and I were having a pillow fight and it got accidentally broken. It <u>was</u> an accident which I understood but she didn't say sorry, instead she just shouted "Well! You started it!" and flounced out of my bedroom. I was gutted. One minute we were playing happily then she just turned sour on me.

This summer was to bring Mum down again. Her lack of discipline confused us and my tantrums accelerated to a different level. Her illness made it harder for her personally to cope with us. I would slam doors so hard they would be near to coming off their hinges and would have to be repaired. My screaming fits were uncontrollable. The anger inside me was raging. I would jump up and down on the floor like a mad person, arms waving about the place. I could be heard down the street and to be honest I became a bit of a nuisance to the next door neighbours. They eventually moved to the empty house over the road. It was said they moved because of me, which is just what you need to make you feel even more at fault! I was told repeatedly that if I carried on I would go back in to care and that I was making Mum ill.

We were packed off one summer afternoon to Aunty Jane's house to give Mum a break. Mrs Beech was informed of where we were and came to pick us up when it was time to go home. Aunty Jane said we had been naughty for Mum so she had taken us for a couple of hours to give her a break. En-route back home, Mrs Beech spoke to us firmly and said we needed to start helping out and behaving ourselves. A lot of pressure was put on us to not make Mum ill. She also helped Mum to reduce her inconsistency in managing us, by advising her on how to better control difficult situations. She needed to be firmer. Things settled down once we were back at school in September and my tempers lessened.

Aunty Jane was a lady who Mum had met at one of the churches she had been to. I grew quite attached to her. I adored her and she adored me. I found in her someone I could go to when I needed the love I craved. She talked to me and made me feel 'normal'. She occupied me with colouring books, stencils and pens. I sat at her kitchen table and watched her make gravy for a roast dinner she was preparing one day and on another day picked blackcurrants from the bush in her back garden. She would always give me a treat like a strawberry split or a packet of crisps and Poppet or Treasure were her nicknames for me. I loved it here and I loved her. I felt relaxed and I could be myself in a normal family environment.

In November the headmaster telephoned Mrs Beech to report a minor incident. He was aware of our history and felt it was necessary. Tracey and I had had a big fight the night before (which sisters do) and it had ended up with us not going to bed until late. From what I remember of this fight it was just a stupid argument. Tracey was winding me up, which she frequently did, and threw an ornament at me. I'd retaliated by walloping her one and had accidentally scratched her face. I had then refused to switch my lamp off, although I can't remember why, so Mum took the bulb out of it. End of!!.... so you would think!

The next morning however, it all got out of hand again. We were all upset and ended up not getting to school on time. Mum took us in to explain our early morning absence to the headmaster and that was the end of it.

A few visits from Mrs Beech were made over the next couple of weeks leading in to December, which saw no major disturbances. Mum came across as happy and said that I was being very helpful at home. I really wanted to be good so I used to make her cups of tea and dust the living room or clean the bathrooms for some pocket money. I used to buy smelly rubbers with my earnings.

As usual, Christmas brought with it much excitement. Plans and preparations had been made for the festive season. Mum cooked a gorgeous roast dinner on the day, with rich, home made gravy.

She comically said, "I'm not making that gravy again, it was too sickly."

I remember receiving a bedside table and an ornament to add to my growing collection. One of the neighbours gave me a bottle of French lavender perfume. You know the way smells remind you of something? Whenever I smell French lavender it reminds me of that particular Christmas.

Mum accepted an invitation to join friends on Boxing Day. I watched Star Wars, which was the big Christmas film on TV that year, whilst the other family's children fixed jigsaws together happily. This family appeared so calm.

Despite all this festive fun Mum was starting to feel down again over Christmas but had kept it to herself. She was afraid of going to hospital again in case we had to go into care again. She must have mentioned it to me at some stage because I had said I was going to kill myself if I had to go away again. Unfortunately though, another spell in care was deemed imminent.

5. Not Again!!

With Christmas over the New Year dawned. At least we still had the pantomime to look forward to. Arrangements had been made by the Social Services department for us to go to the Floral Pavilion at the end of the month. Mrs Beech called in to finalise the details and found Mum to be low. Mum always did get like this when the party season was over and came down with a bang, so to speak. She hadn't contacted Mrs Beech about her feelings due to her fear of us being taken in to care again, or so she said. This was despite being reminded on many occasions that we would only go back in to care if absolutely necessary.

A friend of Mums from the local church, Aunty Lizzy, called to see us whilst Mrs Beech was there. We made a fuss of her and took her upstairs to see our spotless bedrooms. Mrs Beech was well aware of the support that Mum received from friends and family, but couldn't help wonder if many of her anxieties were in fact attention seeking. When we came downstairs we were told about the pantomime and I asked "How much will it cost?" Mrs Beech told me not to worry; we didn't have to pay. She offered Mum a ticket too, as she could not afford it.

Mum telephoned on 24th January requesting an, immediate visit as she was *'in a mess'*. Throughout January several visits were made because Mum felt she could not cope. She wasn't sleeping well and complained that we played up at bed times. She was resting in the day and cleaning the house at night. I recall the Hoover going constantly. The house was always absolutely spotless. You could have eaten your dinner off the floor. Mum wanted the help but again needed reassurance that we would not be taken in to care, and so the home-makers were brought in again to support her during the evenings. Her doctor was also contacted and a visit arranged. Poor Aunty Jane being her good friend was too scared to leave her on her own because she was so distressed.

The day of the pantomime arrived, along with yet another visit from Mrs Beech and another lady from Social Services. Mum became distressed again mid-conversation and so a night-sitter was organised to sit in with her. It crossed Mrs Beech's mind that Mum's obsessive attitude over us not going in to care could have been her actually saying, "Take the children off my hands", however we were taken to the pantomime and had the time of our lives. We were bought sweets and Mrs Beech noted that we were polite and had good manners. When we returned home later the homemaker settled us to bed and sat with Mum chatting until 4 o'clock in the morning. Mum was then back up at 6am.

Two days later Mum was admitted to hospital again, leaving us hysterical. *Not again!!*

A young couple from Emmanuel church took us in for the weekend, on the proviso that at the beginning of the week the home-makers would take over. Mum was very organised about the whole episode, jotting lists and making sure all her finances were in order which seems very strange considering how ill she was meant to be! She also made arrangements to have her benefits picked up at the post office. On admission to hospital she was calm and was happy that all would be well with us. We stayed at Uncle Bill's and Aunty Lizzy's; they were lovely to us. My sister reminded me only recently how they made us shredded wheat in hot milk and the bed we slept in was held up with books. We couldn't move any of them in case it collapsed!

On the 1st February 1983, and back home with one of the home-makers. I busied myself making the tea. My effort was considered to be dominant. In fact I was probably just getting on with it as I was used to taking on this role at home anyway. I often made the tea to help out and in my eagerness to please. Mostly I cooked turkey burgers, instant mash, gravy and peas. *Me and my gravy ay*!! Gammon steaks were also a favourite. I also at some point had switched a light off that the home-maker had put on and this also gave her the impression that I was domineering. I had innocently switched it off being conscious of the usage of electricity as Mum was so thrifty, always watching the pennies. She would always switch lights off after her and was careful with her funds. It had simply rubbed off on me, that was all. Mums finances seemed to be at the forefront of her mind again, even in hospital. Obsessively so!

On 7th February her concerns over a giro prompted a visit from Mrs Beech. Mum looked better but we had *'got on her nerves'* when visiting so she declined another visit from us until she felt well enough. She and the social worker discussed the bills and how much money would need to be given to the home-maker for our keep. Mum said all she could afford was £12 a week for our food.

Considering a lot of money had been spent on material things for our house Mrs Beech's opinion was that her priorities were very wrong. She delicately suggested to Mum that now the house was suitably furnished maybe any extra money could be spent on us all for trips etc. Mum's reply was that she needed a lawn mower and the house was to be decorated. She also was not happy with the attitude of the hospital staff towards her.

The next week Mrs Beech brought along a student to see Mum. She was on a ten week placement and her goal was to improve our behaviour and Mum's confidence in disciplining us. Mum's main interest was her money troubles again. She pondered whether it was wise to go home, yet was unsure if she could cope. Mrs Beech left the student to chat with Mum and called to see us at home. We were planning a welcome home tea and were making posters for her. She asked us how we were going to help Mum out when she came home but we avoided having to answer her questions. I personally felt under a lot of pressure to behave perfectly or I would make Mum ill again.

Mum's stay in hospital lasted nearly three weeks. We hadn't been told she was coming home because of our unruly behaviour the night before for the home-maker. Maybe if she had told us the good news it would have given us the incentive to make the effort. I was annoyed she didn't tell us and we didn't get to bake a cake for Mum because the homemaker was so worn out with us. She commented "No wonder Mum got to the end of her tether," again making me think that everything was my fault. Nevertheless, Mum was welcomed home with open arms but soon she was back into her routine of cleaning the house at night and resting in the day. Mrs Beech called five days later and tried to help but advice from the doctor, community nurse and Mrs Beech all fell upon deaf ears. We were being good but Mum still felt she needed a lot of support and she came across as being hostile towards those trying to help her. One of those trying to help was a home-maker called Emily. Emily was to report Mum as being *'manipulative and hostile'*.

Occasionally, Mum allowed us to stay home from school as she did not want to be on her own. This undermined what the student and home-makers were trying to do with us as a family. Mum had been up cleaning through the night again and so we had all slept in one morning in February. Mrs Beech called round concerned about this; Mum was not very co-operative and remained silent for most of the visit. Mrs Beech noticed my confusion at her ignorance. We made a fuss of Mum and were being very good as we could see she was depressed. At this point Emily arrived and tried to reason with Mum too, but this just aggravated mum and she left the room. Mum was adamant that she wasn't getting enough help and that she needed someone to be with her at night. It was thought that if the level of help was not enough then maybe hospital was the best place for her.

Emily's efforts did her no favours and from this point on Mum had a big problem with her, making complaints which were felt unjust by Social Services. Even Aunty Jane considered taking a back seat for a while, as she felt Mum was out of order too. For the next month it was Emily that occupied Mum's mind and not our behaviour for a change. Mum eventually resigned herself to coping without the home-makers at all as she believed everyone to be in cahoots with each other and she would not listen to reason. Mum was completely oblivious to all the help and support she had had from people over the years and was intent on dwelling on her misunderstanding with Emily. Emily had said the wrong thing to Mum and she just couldn't let it go. The student had not been able to carry out her goals now due to Mums lack of co-operation.

By April it was clear that I was helping Mum to cope in place of the home-makers and was taking on the parenting role. I was now doing some shopping and cleaning for Mum and cooking the meals for Tracey and me. When in her depressed frame of mind I remember more than once Mum locking herself in her bedroom and barricading the door up with furniture so no one could get in. She would be in there for days at a time and we were left to fend for ourselves. I made cups of tea and sat them outside her bedroom door. I'd knock and let her know it was there sometimes leaving little messages or notes for her. She would tell me repeatedly that she was a failure, 'no good' or that we were better off without her. She would say she was a burden to people and never to trust anyone because 'they all drop you'. I used to have to talk her out of overdosing saying how much we loved her and pointing out all the good things she did have to live for.

Through May and June Mum complained that I was getting out of control. In such a confusing environment was it any wonder? A lot of the time my sister would wind me up knowing I had a short fuse. When I snapped this was the desired reaction and more often than not I would get the blame for retaliating. Mum and Mrs Beech were well aware of Tracey teasing me but still I always ended up the one in trouble. Members of Emmanuel Church had tried to help by planning a rota of baby sitters for Mum so she could go to church meetings and get out of the house at bit more.

It was my eleventh birthday. I would be leaving Green bank Junior School this summer and going to my new secondary school in September. My Nan took me out to get my ears pierced but we couldn't find anywhere that did it. We walked and walked down the country lanes to the next set of shops but to no avail. We never really spent that much time with Nan and Granddad. I think they found Mum too difficult to cope with and had taken a step back.

Nan wasn't my real Nan; she wasn't my Mum's real Mum. She was my Granddads second wife, and I don't think her and Mum ever quite got on. There had been times when we had visited them or stayed with them and gone to the park with Aunty Una (Mum's half sister). We came from a large family and had a lot of cousins but now we didn't really see any of them anymore.

There were also times in the past when Mum had taken us for walks and told us stories. She made them up as she went along about pixies and fairies and elves. We loved the stories and we kicked and crunched through autumn leaves on our travels whilst listening intently, but those days were gone now. I always remember of these walks trying desperately to hold on to Mum's hand, which mostly had all the properties of a wet lettuce. My pleas to her of "hold my hand mummy, hold my hand," were always met with "I'm too tired".

I entered a, "Make, bake and grow" competition

around this time. I took a cardboard box and transformed it in to a Sindy caravan, complete with wallpaper, curtains and a folding bed made from old bits of material and shoe boxes. It had a sink and windows. I even had plasticine chips, egg and peas on a Sindy plate. I made such an effort and worked very hard on it. I won first prize for my effort and my picture was in the local paper.

Over the last two years I had become quite fond of the Sunday school teacher, Martin, from Emmanuel Church. He was friends with Mum and the nearest thing Tracey and I had to a father figure. We had all been away with the church for a weekend that April and we had a lot of fun with him. He had chased me around a field one day with a hose pipe and I laughed uncontrollably as he soaked me with it. He also was a fan of Cliff Richard and we would all sing together at our house to the records we loved so much. He had joined in with the rota that was made up for babysitting and took us to the beach one night when it was his turn. We spent a lot of time with him and he was good to Mum too. I learned an awful lot about the Christian faith from him on Sunday mornings. I'd memorised verses and won prizes. I still have the verses in my bible now. One of the verses I had memorised was, 'For God so loved the world, that He gave His only begotten Son, that whosoever believeth in Him should not perish, but have everlasting life' (*John 3:16*). I believed in Him. It was when I was eleven that I prayed to God at the back of our church in the service one Sunday morning and I gave my life to God. I wanted to be a good person and I wanted to be forgiven for my sins. Becoming a Christian didn't make my life any easier. In fact I sometimes think it makes life harder.

Not Again!!

I loved Uncle Martin and I was broken hearted after what he and Mum liaised to do together. I can't even remember what I had done (probably being cheeky) but I was in trouble for something. Mum's great idea was to get Uncle Martin to punish me as she thought I might take notice of him, he being a man and our only father figure. I was being told off by him and Mum. I'll be honest I was a gob-on-a-stick at this age and I probably was quite defiant. Uncle Martin then proceeded to put me over his knee and give me a good hiding. I screamed the place down. Oh my gosh! Why was Uncle Martin hitting me? I lashed out at Mum in frustration striking her leg as by this time I was on the floor in my struggle to get away. Why was she letting him do this to me? I looked towards her for help. I was eleven and extremely embarrassed. Mum just looked on with a face of stone. Then it dawned on me, she had put him up to it.

Uncle Martin and I were never the same again after that. I walked away from him that day in June. He tried to apologise to me but I was too embarrassed and hurt, not physically but emotionally. I could see he was wracked with guilt but I ignored him even more to punish him back for what he had done to me. I have never forgotten that awful moment in my life.

Mum had contacted the police and Social Services after the incident in the hope that just I would be taken in to care. I'd been walloped and lost Uncle Martin but it still wasn't enough punishment. I cried when the subject of going back in to care was brought up when Mrs Beech arrived to discuss what had happened. Mrs Beech told Mum it was unfair to single me out as it would make me feel resentful and rejected. Tracey and I were both told that it was up to us now as well as Mum if we wanted to avoid going back in to care. Mum had been hysterical earlier on but later became quite calm and decided to take me shopping leaving Tracey to go to school. The headmaster and social worker concluded it was not surprising there was a wedge being driven between us and no wonder that I was confused and lashing out at Mum.

On the 24th June our concerned headmaster telephoned Mrs Beech. We were not at school again. She called to our house to find us all in bed. We came downstairs on her arrival and I told her that we were OK, but "Mummy did not want us to go to school today".

Mum was completely incoherent towards Mrs Beech. Mum had become far too reliant on members of the church community, waking them in the early hours of the morning, wanting someone to sit with her and not wanting them to go home. She used to go 'walkabout' at all hours of the night whilst we were asleep in bed, leaving us home alone. Her friends felt obliged to escort her back home and Uncle Bill had visited Mum saying, "Enough is enough".

Mum was very upset at this (her reason for keeping us with her that day). Uncle Bill also expressed his concern for Uncle Martin whom Mum had become heavily reliant on. Although the church had not completely withdrawn their support, Mum felt as though she was being rejected by them. Mrs Beech pointed out that perhaps her behaviour was unreasonable and discussed this at great length with her. During the conversation Tracey and I showered her with love and attention, Tracey made tea and toast and I climbed on to her knee and put my arms around her.

Not Again!!

We fussed around her but got absolutely nothing back. The report of the meeting said she was *'completely self centred'*.

Mrs Beech informed the headmaster of our reason for absence. They were both united in their concern for us having to cope with Mum's self-pity and apparent lack of insight into our emotional needs.

Meanwhile, bad news was on its way from Wales which was sure to rock the boat even more. Mum was to be informed that great Granddad in Chirk had sadly passed away.

6. A Death in the Family

Uncle Bill broke the news to Mum of Great Granddads death and the church rallied around to support us. Mum was still very angry and upset with Bill because of his so called rejection and his efforts of support were shown no gratitude. On Mrs Beech's home visit she sympathised with Mum for the loss of our Granddad but mum's concerns lay with me and what was going to be done about me. As usual I was getting the blame for causing trouble. I admit I did used to punch Tracey on the back repeatedly in frustration when she riled me. Mum again asked for me to be singly taken in to care oblivious to the fact that Tracey had a lot to do with my resentment and anger. Tracey was Mum's blue eyed girl and she played on this getting me in to trouble. Don't get me, wrong I hold nothing against Tracey for this. We both did what we had to do for Mum's attention. Mrs Beech once more pointed out that it was not fair to single me out. If care was necessary it should be for both of us. Clearly she could see what was happening.

Granddads funeral took place in Chirk at the end of June. We stayed with Aunty Jane when Mum attended the funeral. The next day however she didn't turn up to collect us and the police had to be notified. Granddads death had hit her hard. It was now essential for us to be placed in care.

A Death in the Family

We packed our things and were placed with a foster family just up the road. At least this meant we could stay at our same school and be near our friends. We were excited to go to our new family and didn't show any upset. Maybe we were just getting used to it. At our new foster home I immediately settled well becoming very cooperative and responding well to the discipline. I was much happier and contented in this normal family environment. Tracey on the other hand was clearly not happy with the firm handling and was harder to please. I was very pleased to see Mrs Beech when she called to see us on the 6th July. I told her it was great here and that I hadn't even had time to play with my Barbie dolls as there was so much to do. I asked about Mum and was told that she was ill again and back in hospital after Granddads death. She hadn't asked about us… or for us to visit her.

I was told that Uncle Bill had visited her and I passed comment on how he had the cheek to, after what he had said to Mum. I suppose I didn't really understand the situation. Mrs Beech noted how Mum told us too much and involved us in her problems. She also noticed that we hadn't asked about Mum until she had mentioned her. When she left I gave Mrs Beech a kiss goodbye. She saw this as a clear indication that I was happy and relieved to be free of my responsibilities at home.

In mid-July we visited Mum in hospital. It was her birthday. She had a beautiful birthday cake with green and white butter icing on it. It tasted delicious. We took home-made birthday cards and flowers for her. We sang happy birthday to her and I cried as I clung on to her. I remember feeling uneasy in the hospital setting and desperately wanted Mum to come home.

There were some really strange people on the wards. One elderly lady I noticed was unnervingly hovering around us. Suddenly the lady saw her chance and snatched at the birthday cake sitting on Mums knee. She legged it down the corridor stuffing mounds of the sweet sponge in to her mouth. Mum said she hadn't been allowed the cake and that's why she had grabbed it and ran. We stayed with Mum for a little while and thanked Mrs Beech for taking us to see her when we left.

Certainly our new Foster Parents observed our behaviour and it was found to be Tracey who caused the problems at bedtimes and not me. She had also tried to get their three year old son in to trouble. This wasn't so much a problem but the Foster Parents, Aunty Joan and Uncle Mike, said they couldn't work her out and she was difficult at times. I became very defensive and protective of Tracey while we were here. We ganged up together against authority unlike at home where we argued a lot. On the whole though I was able to show my nice side and the only real problem with me was a particular morning when I refused to go to school and I was packing my bags to go back home. Mrs Beech came and had a chat with me and I listened to her advice to go to school. Problem solved!

Aunty Joan and Uncle Mike took us along on their family holiday to Anglesey. I remember staying in a caravan. I had a huge tantrum when we got there because I didn't want to share a bedroom with Tracey. Our bedtime routine had improved tremendously since staying with our Foster Parents. I was worried that she would get me in to trouble again at night. I remember kicking and screaming about it but they left me to get on with it and afterwards when I had calmed down it was no longer an issue. It wasn't even mentioned to the social worker. We enjoyed the holiday, spending a lot of time on the beach. I remember swimming in the pool at night and buying a piggy ornament to take back home as a souvenir.

We stayed for a month with Aunty Joan and Uncle Mike and returned back home after the holiday in Anglesey. It didn't take long for the bedtime shenanigans to start again!

We had another trip away again with the church a few weeks later: a weekend in the Cotswolds. Mum was depressed at the beginning of the holiday and people were worried about her. Never the less we had a great time and I learned to swim properly and dive in the swimming pool that was on the grounds. I had had swimming lessons at my school but was so lacking in confidence that I had failed.

Back home when asking how the holiday had gone Mrs Beech commented on how Mums depression could have spoilt the holiday for us and other concerned parties. Again she noted how Mum came across as completely self-centred and was unconcerned how it affected us. She also reported how she believed it was an impossible task to change anything and that probably nothing was likely to change.

In September, Mrs Beech visited us and was concerned to learn that we had slept in bed with Mum the night before as she was feeling so down and *'in a state'*. I had school that day and was tired from lack of sleep. Mrs Beech expressed her concern for the effect Mum's depression was having on us. She wasn't really listening and her reply was: "We're all in this together, who else is there to help?"

Help? If twenty six visits from January to June isn't help then I don't know what is!

Now that it was September there was more change on the agenda for me: I started my new secondary school. Prior to this, Mum had sat with me and told me about the birds and the bees. She was very thorough in giving me a prep talk about periods and boys and feelings. I felt quite close to Mum at times like these.

I remember how daunting that first day of school was. Not knowing my way around and being smaller than everyone else. I was above average intelligence but was put in one of the lower forms. I settled in well and was considered to be a friendly, pleasant girl and very artistic.

By December things got really bad again. Mum was still not sleeping and finding the nights hard to deal with. She had telephoned the police one night. I was extremely worried about her and when Mrs Beech called my concern was obvious to her. She tried to talk to Mum but again she was incoherent and awkward. Any suggestions were frowned upon. She asked if the home-makers were still available and it was suggested to her that she see her doctor if she felt bad enough to need their assistance.

Mum refused, saying "No way are the children going in care ever again."

Mrs Beech came to the conclusion that Mum was shutting her out, just as she had with the home-makers last year.

Mid December, Mum requested hospitalisation. She said she was upset nobody had been to see her this particular week. She was very depressed and said she could not cope with Christmas. I'm not sure why she felt that way as Mum has always been well organised and preparations had always been made early, so there was nothing to stress about.

An appointment had been made for Mrs Beech to see Mum on the 15th December but when she arrived no one was at home. She waited a while and then I arrived home from school and waited with her. Mum was at Tracey's school collecting her. She had told the headmaster she felt like overdosing so had come to get Tracey to avoid being on her own in the house and doing so. The worried headmaster brought her home with Tracey and relayed this information back to Mrs Beech. Mum knew Mrs Beech was coming that afternoon, so hadn't needed to go out to avoid being on her own. It came to light that Mum had had several calls from friends that week too even though she said she'd had none. Mrs Beech was baffled.

On the 19th December, six days before Christmas Mum did take an overdose. She was taken to hospital in the middle of the night. We were uprooted and taken to Aunty Jane's till the next day. All I can remember is coming home from school the next day and feeling really ill. I walked the long stretch of road wanting to be sick. I felt as if I'd had an accident in my pants and I couldn't wait to get to the loo. I got home and desperately ran straight to the toilet. I had started my first period. I cried with relief and thought that all my anger would go away now as this must have been the cause of my frustrations. I was turning in to a woman! I ran out of the

From Care to Somewhere

toilet needing to tell someone. This should have been a mother and daughter moment, but she wasn't there to tell. I excitedly shouted my news to the home-maker who was busy chatting to Mrs Beech and she said "Oh, OK then" and dismissed me without a thought. I was gutted.

We put the Christmas tree up that evening and carried on as normal but all the while Christmas would be tainted if Mum wasn't at home. Mum did come home for Christmas a few days later but she was still very unhappy.

We fussed around Mrs Beech a few days after Christmas, showing off our presents. Tracey acted daft and had us in stitches. Mum was very restrained and did her best not to laugh at her. Mrs Beech felt that it was very hard for us with Mum and was at a loss to know how to help anymore.

A few days after that Mum started refusing visitors. She would send one of us to the door to tell them she wasn't well. She would stay in bed for hours and not get up. We were left to get on with it. One of the homemakers was sent in on 4th January to help and offered to take us all out. Mum stayed in bed and Tracey went out with her but I refused to go in case Mum needed me for anything. In fact, I was frightened to leave her in case she overdosed again. Then it would be my fault for leaving her alone.

The social worker and home-makers were all very disheartened at this stage. Mum had a kind of power over people and was very manipulative. She had gone from one extreme to another and the threat of her 'taking too many tablets' meant that people were now having to tread on egg shells with her, watching what they said and not pushing her in fear of her doing something stupid. Mum kept saying to me "you're better off without me." I always took this to mean she was contemplating suicide and I would try to persuade her otherwise.

On the 7th January 1984 Mum was taken back in to hospital as an emergency case. I can only assume she did take another overdose. Tracey and I were placed in a Children's home for day care over the weekend and homemakers stayed with us at home overnight. This was a short term arrangement and we went home soon afterwards. Edge Hill Children's Home would become my home later that year.

7. Young Love

It became increasingly difficult for Mrs Beech to remain as our social worker. Mum criticised her for giving us attention and not enough to her. Mrs Beech tried once again to get Mum to see how her erratic behaviour was affecting us but to no avail. When people tried to do anything to help, Mum was deeply offended. If the wrong thing was said she habitually blew things out of all proportion. She complained that she didn't get any help and Mrs Beech had now upset her too. A similar situation to that of Emily the year before ensued. I remember Mum complaining about her and telling me that Mrs Beech would ask her "How can I help you?"

Mum was annoyed that Mrs Beech didn't seem to know how to help her. All her suggestions had been frowned upon. Mrs Beech had been our social worker for two and a half years but now Mum would refuse to have her "over the doorstep."

I met Andrea at my new school, who it turned out only lived up the road from me. She and I became good friends in the summer. I often went to her house and her parents seemed to like me and accept me into their fold. Andrea and I used to take their two dogs for walks and we had so much fun together. One of the dogs walked really fast and the other really slow. Andrea looked comical walking sideways with them her arms outstretched, one dog in front and the other behind. Her Dad gave me an old purple bike and said I could have it if I wasn't offended.

Offended? I was chuffed!

Her Mum introduced me to raw mushrooms on a salad she made for us one day. Eeeew! Raw mushrooms, I thought, but I gave them a try and they were lovely. Raw mushrooms to this day always remind me of Andrea.

We spent hours riding around together and we used to cut through all the public foot paths and fields. One day we stopped off in a cow field and climbed up a big tree. The cows were miles away when we first got there but then before we'd noticed it they were under the branch that we were sitting in. My usually sensible and quiet friend gave no warning as to what she did next. I couldn't believe it when she jumped out of the tree and on to an unsuspecting cow's back. She galloped half way across the field hanging on to its tail. Hilarious!

I turned twelve in June. Not long after, I met my first boyfriend. He was fifteen and gorgeous. He had a, wedged style haircut and his ear was pierced three times.

I was in the park on my bike and had stopped for a go on the swing and all I heard from behind me was "Wow! Hiya gorgeous!"

I turned around to see this handsome boy admiring my sun kissed hair. He was fascinated by all the streaks and asked me how I'd got it like that. He asked me to go out with him and so I did. We sat and talked on the skate ramps in the park and I would spend time with him at his house. He would make me a salad sandwich and we went for walks in the park by the waterfall. I had my first kiss there in the park. He lent me his Paul Young and Thomson Twins tapes. The butterflies in my stomach made me feel sick and I lost my appetite. I would ride to his house on my bike and spent every moment I could with him.

Aahh, young love!

Our three month relationship was completely innocent. Mum wasn't happy about it at all though. I really don't know why, I had done nothing wrong. She was totally unreasonable and blew everything out of proportion. At first she wanted me to invite him for tea so she could meet him but I would have been mortified if anything embarrassing had happened at home, so I didn't ask him and it never happened. She grounded me and told me to stop seeing him and then took my bike away so I couldn't ride to his house anymore. There were no reasons why. No compromises. I defied her and I tried to take my bike back. She had put it upstairs and I wrestled it back down them. I was shocked when she shouted "You little bitch!" because Mum didn't usually swear.

I was confused One minute Mum was in bed threatening suicide and I was being the parent; now she wanted to control me all of a sudden. So many mixed messages over the years had brought it to this. I walked out of the house telling her what time I would be in. In the midst of our row I was still trying to be reasonable but I was not going to be controlled.

That night, the 20th August 1984, I was taken to the children's home. Mum had phoned the police and our social worker saying she couldn't cope with me and may harm me. Mum threatened to put me in a home on many occasions before if I didn't change but I never believed for a second that she would actually do it.

We had a new social worker by now, Mrs Peabody. I hated her at the time and I could tell she hated me too. As far as I was concerned she had come into a situation she knew nothing about. She just saw me as an angry, aggressive, horrible teenager. Well, that's how I felt she thought of me anyway!

A meeting was held at Edge Hill so that recent developments could be discussed. Mum immediately complained about losing her money because I wasn't at home and she wanted to know who was responsible for kitting me out now. Bedtimes were discussed and a plan was drawn up of when I could see my boyfriend, although they needn't have bothered because we had split up anyway. I mean who wants to go visit their girlfriend in a children's home?

On the plus side I was to get pocket money here. **Yippee!** I went shopping and bought pink hair gel and the *Smash Hits* magazine.

At another meeting Mum took me to one side and told me that she needed me to come home. She said her money had been stopped for me and she could no longer afford for me to stay in care. She asked me to promise to be good and then she would arrange for me to go back home. I was happy to go home but very sad that it was only because she needed the money. This is something that sticks out vividly in my mind. Anyway, she changed her mind a few days later saying I had been making demands on her and she didn't want me to go home after all. I had called in one day to say hello to her whilst visiting a friend up that way and she later phoned the home complaining about it.

I hadn't made any demands at all, I knew Mum had no money, why would I?

Then she cancelled a visit to see me for the same reason. I felt extremely let down.

Mum criticised me further by saying I was playing with a girl who swears (I was banned from seeing her too) and that I had written a note with swear words on it. These were all trivial things that most children do but in my case Mum totally exaggerated every situation. I became bitterly angry and confused. Tracey had been bought new clothes now I'd gone and I was left out. Why didn't Mum want me? She was now blaming me for being in care, blaming my behaviour. Id never been in trouble with the police or drank or smoked. I hadn't really been all that bad, up until now...

I had been grounded for something at the home and I tried to get out of the house, but there were locks on the windows. I took a pair of scissors and used the pointy end of them to unscrew the locks and I defiantly threw them down the toilet! A member of staff followed me up the stairs to retrieve the scissors I had taken and I told her to get away from me, brandishing the scissors at her. I then sat on the window ledge with my legs hanging out of the open window and threatened to jump. I had turned in to a nut case!

Another incident at the home saw me smashing my stiletto shoe in to a girls face. In this instance I was defending myself. The girl and her sister had been picking on me for quite a while until I snapped. I hit her with my shoe and ran screaming from the room in a panic thinking "They're going to kill me now!" They didn't come near me again after that. I did make some friends in the home and the staff became like aunties and uncles but I had learned to distance myself from people. Save getting hurt when they left!

The plan amongst the authorities and Mum was to wean me home gradually and so weekend stays were introduced. Mum blew hot and cold. One minute everything was fine for me to go, the next she didn't want to see me at all. I built my hopes up and then they were dashed.

I asked her many times, "What have I done wrong?"

Or I would say, "Tell me what I've done wrong so I can put it right."

She would never answer me. At another meeting Mum made out there had been trouble at home when really there hadn't.

I shouted at her in anger, "you're going round the bend and you're a liar!"

"Why can't I be like other kids?"

In October I was dropped off at home by staff for the weekend even though I was quite positive there were no plans for this particular weekend. When I got there it turned out I was right. Mum kicked off as I had turned up unannounced. I left after a row about it. It was a mistake on the home's behalf and I was treated unfairly.

Nevertheless I was discharged from care and went back home on 26th November as Mum couldn't cope financially without me. Great!

I had always suffered with my chest at home and I sneezed an awful lot. I seemed to permanently have a mound of toilet roll wedged up my nostrils. It was thought I was having an allergic reaction to something. I was referred to a hospital in Liverpool for some tests. I had to have thirty six needles pricked in to my right arm with various substances blobbed on to each puncture mark. The ones that bubbled up went very itchy and showed that I was reacting to grass pollen, three types of bedroom dust and cat fur. It was our cat that was making me sneeze and my eyes itch furiously.

Mum wasn't happy and said, *"were not getting rid of the cat because of you."* I didn't blame her though really because I loved kitty too.

I had only been back at home for two months when it all went belly up again. I really don't even know what I'd done. Mum phoned Mrs Peabody saying I had been up at midnight the night before moving my furniture around in the bedroom. The next day she arrived at our house to take me away again. Mum just carried on doing the dishes and was totally distant. I remember Mrs Peabody phoning another social worker for assistance to remove me from home. When he arrived, I ran up the stairs and locked myself in the bathroom. He tried to turn the lock from the outside but I was very strong. There was no way I was going back to care. My behaviour may have been unruly but it didn't justify this. He was there for a while trying to unlock the door and eventually retreated, or so

I thought. He went to look for a screwdriver, came back and forced the lock with all his strength. I couldn't hold it anymore and it turned in my hand. He may have opened the door but I still wouldn't budge from the bathroom. The police were then involved and I was escorted to Mrs Peabody's car. The man that unlocked the bathroom sat in the passenger seat and I was sat behind him when I flipped my lid. I kicked at him and punched and screamed. I hated them. I didn't punch at Mrs Peabody though because she was driving the car and I didn't want to cause an accident. Very thoughtful of me!

I was admitted to Edge Hill Children's Home again on 6th February 1985. This time I just got on with it. I gave up trying. There was the same routine of meetings and trying to resolve problems. Another of my weekend visits was cancelled because Mum couldn't afford to have me home. More complaints about her finances and problems arose with Mrs Peabody herself and yet another member of staff that had said something to upset her.

I was at home on a visit one day and had made a pot of tea. I picked it up to pour the tea and slopped it on the floor. It was an accident! Mum shouted at me: "Get back to care!" She admitted to taking things out on me to Mrs Peabody. Apart from this incident visits had gone really well and Mum stated that she did want me to come home.

I had settled in to Edge Hill this time around. It was just like a big family; well at least they tried to make it feel that way. At home I had used to find solace in my Enid Blyton books but I hadn't brought them with me to the home. Things had a habit of going missing in these places. Even your socks!

They had these great big cushions in the living area at the home that we piled up in to a huge cushion mountain. We nestled in to them and settled down and watched *Willy Wonka and the Chocolate Factory.* It was magical. There was a stereo in a back room too. I remember an excited Aunty Edie (one of the staff) charging in on hearing Stevie Wonder's *I Just Called to Say I Love You.* To say she liked it was an understatement! Uncle Kev took a few of us blackberry picking one day. He ate egg butties and banana together and said, *"mmm quite nice that,"* and I thought Eeeee!

The staff let me bake a cake one day too. I accidentally used custard powder instead of flour as the labels on the tins weren't very clear. I thought I was going to get told off but it was fine. The cake tasted lovely while it was still hot but it was very dry and powdery when it cooled down. Another time aunty Edie let me make risotto. I had seen her make it and thought "Yeah, I can do that," No I couldn't; my effort was a crimson pan of sludge. Gross!

I returned home in May. We did have some OK times in the periods that I was back at home. Sometimes we would all laugh uncontrollably till our stomachs hurt and I would make every one howl with my chicken impressions. There was no happy medium. Mum was either high as a kite or in the depths of despair.

Mum and I sang in a choir at the Philharmonic Hall. It was something to do with the church and we performed in front of a full audience. We also went to the Billy Graham crusade at Anfield and sang at that. That was

Young Love

a great experience and I confirmed my Christian belief here

One day I was helping Mum out in the garden. I playfully tipped water over her bare feet when she was watering the plants. I was just having fun and thought Mum would see the funny side. Then she tripped over me. OK, I had gone too far!

The next day Mum went on and on about it. She said I had done it on purpose and it ended up in a row and her telling me: "Get out and don't bother coming back!" I went to school, not sure if I would be allowed home or not. Our latest social worker, George, arrived and he smoothed things over. *No more Mrs Peabody!* She didn't last long!

George was a lovely man who took a gentle approach with us. He organised for us to go to a play-scheme in the summer holidays and suggested that a holiday may benefit us. Mum didn't want to take me on holiday though, only Tracey.

At some later stage we were having a row over something and Mum bashed me straight over the head with a big wooden tray. I remained fixed where I was and forced myself to show no reaction. I thought that's what she wanted from me and then she would have an excuse to get rid of me again. I stood there rooted to the spot motionless. The tray split in half.

She also took a carpet beater to me once. I grabbed at it as it swung towards me and I twisted the canes in my hand, damaging it. No way was she hitting me with that thing.

Mum had had enough of me again and I was admitted to care again on 19th July. A different home this time, Wimbrick Hey Assessment Centre. I was there for a weekend. On admission I was told to have a bath and then I had to stand naked with my legs apart and was checked for signs of physical abuse. I didn't want to do it but I was told I had no choice. I found this humiliating to say the very least.

Mr Dennis, our old social worker from years ago had taken a job further up the ladder. He found out I had been placed in to care again and gave instructions I was to be taken home immediately as my Mum was simply being manipulative.

8. Another Boyfriend, Another Problem

George visited us in August at Mum's request as a matter of urgency. Mum had got in to one of her states, once again claiming she could no longer cope with me. The thought of me being at home for the holidays aggravated her. George tried to help find a compromise. He suggested it may help if Mum didn't nag me all the time and I agreed to try and curb my temper. He thought the situation was resolved at that.

We were busy showing George our dolls and records and things upstairs when Mum suddenly shouted "I can't stay in this house a minute longer, something has to be done!" and walked out of the house. George was taken aback. He rushed out of the house to her and calmly suggested she wait and see what happened through the next week. Mum agreed but said "I hate her right now."

I hadn't been causing any particular problems. Just a bit of jealousy of Tracey on my behalf, which was understandable, given that I was the one always shoved in to care and not her.

The summer holidays had begun and we went to the play-scheme as organised by George. The following week one of the home-makers helped us to pack our bags and we went on a camping trip. Mum was depressed again and didn't want me to come back home afterwards but I was looking forward to camping and Tracey was coming too. I looked forward to us being together in the tent. We could be proper sisters and do fun things together. No such luck. Tracey was in a different age group so her tent was across the field with the younger ones. I was so disappointed.

I shared my tent with a girl that lived in our road a few doors away and another girl I knew from school. We were desperately trying to pitch our tent. I was there with my hammer and peg, botching it up when I heard "You're doing it wrong."

I turned around and a very handsome young man with silver blonde hair was talking to me. I felt like a damsel in distress being rescued. He came over and took the hammer and did it for me. He was nice!

That night us girls were chatting and having a laugh in our tent. We all lay with our heads sticking out of the tent admiring the view. My rescuer!

One of the girls shouted out "How about a good night kiss then?"

He said, *"ok"* and walked over, bent down and planted a kiss on my lips. Mine, not hers. Well, he hadn't said who he was going to kiss!

I was so flattered. The rest of the week I spent a lot of time with the young man. He walked with me to red rocks and we talked. He liked me, I could tell. His name was Ben and he was sixteen and not bad looking. He turned out to be a helper both with the play-scheme and at Tracey's school.

Another Boyfriend, Another Problem

I didn't really see Tracey all that weekend but I kept on looking out for her. Meanwhile my friends and I played treasure hunts and had midnight walks in the woods. On the last day of camp the girls all egged each other on to jump in the lake, so I did - with all my clothes on. It was freezing. What a nutter!

When we got back home after the weekend's frivolity, I went straight to bed and fell asleep in an instant, absolutely exhausted. Ben stayed in touch with me and it wasn't long before I started seeing him.

Another boyfriend, another problem! The arguments started again. Mum was unhappy at my going out with him and I felt she was totally unreasonable. I was fed up of the rowing and being blamed for making her ill so I'd go out to get out of her way. I admit by now I was rude, aggressive and abusive. I'd had had the blame for being that way for so long that I became that way. I shouted, screamed and was argumentative and I'd now started smoking. Mum and I had yet another row and she threatened to put me in care again. I said I would run away if she tried.

On 30th September I again argued with her that if she was going to put me in care, then I would run away. If she didn't want me anyway, why should she care where I was? I felt that she hated me and just used any excuse to get rid of me. She was adamant that I was going to the home so I pinched all the two pence's off the radiators (that were used to turn the dial) and I ran away. I used the two pence pieces to get the bus and went to meet Ben. Ben, bless him, did the right thing and coaxed me in to going back home that night. It was 11.15 pm when I eventually got back. He had mistakenly thought that by bringing me home it would prove to Mum he was a nice lad and he deserved a chance. It didn't make any difference at all.

The next day, the scene erupted again. Mum phoned George, telling him she could not face another night with me. He came to the house and tried to resolve things with us. I was so angry now at her continual rejection of me that it was beyond discussion. I shouted and argued and ended up running out of the house, thumping Mum out of my way. I ran away again on the 1st October 1985 and I wasn't coming back.

I didn't have much money this time so literally did run, for about three miles, barefoot. I headed towards the estate that Ben lived but didn't go there in case he tried to take me home again. I jumped on a passing bus and went to look for a friend from school. I'd told her I'd thought about running away and she'd said I could go to her house. The only problem was I couldn't find her house and I ended up walking the streets in the dark. I bumped in to a young man and asked him the way to Noctorum. He walked with me and helped me to get there on the condition I gave him a kiss. I was lucky he only wanted a kiss, he could have been anyone. I still couldn't find my friend's house. A group of girls were out in the street and I stopped to ask them for directions but no one knew the way. One of the girls was quite worried about me on my own at that time of night and she let me stay on her mum's sofa for the night.

The next day I started to walk to Birkenhead. I felt really light headed and tired. It's hard to sleep on a stranger's sofa with so much on your mind. I didn't know where I was going to go or where I would find food, but I wasn't going back home. I was soon stopped by a girl asking me for a light. Joanne was fifteen, two years older than me and bunking off school. I told her I'd run away from home. We made friends and I went with her. She was walking into town and knew where to go to get some food. Joanne knew a man in the market and she asked him if he would put me up for the night.

He replied, "Only if you sleep in my bed with me."

Oh my gosh! The pervert! No chance!

We walked around the town for most of the day. Joanne asked her Nan later on that day if I could stay at her house. I slept there on the second night. I hung around the local shops in the day whilst she was at school. On the third night I went to Joanne's house with her. Her Mum was getting a bit suspicious of me and found out that I'd run away. I think my taking a bath must have given it away. I got dressed and came down the stairs.

Joanne said to me "When I say run, run!" and promptly dragged me out of the house with her. She had run away with me. I would never have asked her to do that.

We ran around the corner, caught our breath, then walked on and who should we bump in to but Ben. I tried to avoid him but he had seen me and came straight over. He was worried about me. He was with some friends of his and we hung around for a while. They were nice boys. Later that night we went to one of Joanne's friends who had her own flat and she let us stay there.

The next night Joanne's Mum and Dad came looking for her in their car. I hadn't wanted her to run because of me but I was sad when she got in the car and went back home. Why hadn't my Mum come looking for me? She didn't want me!

For the next three nights I slept rough. I attempted to sleep in a subway and on a bridge going over the railway but that was too windy. All I had on was a little white dress and my mint green top that I'd received on my thirteenth birthday. I had no socks, jelly shoes and just a thin cardigan and I was freezing. I curled up amongst the chip papers and cigarette ends on the ground of a public phone box to sleep but that was uncomfortable. Mostly I just walked around. I washed myself as best I could in the sports centre's toilets and fell asleep in broad daylight on a picnic bench outside the shops because I was so exhausted.

On the last day before I was picked up I woke up on a primary school doorstep when the children were arriving for the day. I quickly moved on.

Later on that night I met up with Ben and his friends and we sat talking. Little did I know that Ben had told the police where I was and they came to fetch me in a place he had suggested to them. The police car pulled up and I knew they had come for me when they started asking questions. I was so tired that I admitted defeat. I needed to have a bath and a sleep. I got in to the police car and they took me home. I could tell by my mums face and her body language from the car window what she had said: "I don't want her, take her back to the children's home."

And that's exactly where I went.

9. The Foster Parents

Apparently my school had prayed for me all week in assembly. Bless them. I loved my school. I was happy here. I had been a Billy No-mates when I'd first started there, but now I was a bit more popular and had two different crowds of friends. My friends accepted me with my problems, just as I was. My teacher and form tutor were brilliant too. I could tell they cared about me because they encouraged me. They bought me Christmas and birthday presents and they saw the good in me. I had been caught smoking once but I was never really bad at school. I was more the class clown than anything else and sometimes I went over the top. I was bubbly in nature and tried to make people laugh so that they would like me.

On the 8th October 1985 I was sent to live with foster parents, Brenda and Matt. I was very subdued at this time and very down. The boys who I had met with Ben came to visit me that weekend and this cheered me up a lot. They seemed to really look out for me but they were a lot older than me. They had fallen out with Ben for telling the police where I was, as had I. I started seeing one of the boys for a while, but I ended it not long after as I felt that he was just a friend, nothing more. He was a lovely lad but I didn't want that kind of relationship with him. He was gutted and walked home in tears punching the swing in the park on his way through. I felt so guilty for hurting him. I didn't see the boys much after that.

I developed really bad stomach pains over the first few days with my new foster parents and a doctor was called out. They thought I was pregnant! The Cheek! I was still innocent in that department and was annoyed that that was what people thought of me. I had to have an examination and a pregnancy test, more humiliation!! The doctor walked out of the bedroom when he had finished and that's when I realised what my pain was. I hung on and waited for the doctor to disappear down the stairs. Then I passed copious amounts of wind. Phew, what a relief!

George arrived to see me at Brenda and Matt's house a few days later, to see if I had settled in OK. They had a nice house. He asked me if I was happy to stay here. I felt awkward. The Foster Parents were there so I felt as though I couldn't refuse. I said yes but really I didn't want to. Stupid me!

Things were good to start with. Brenda and Matt had a daughter of their own and she seemed to be nice at first. Mum didn't want to see me and refused to come to the foster parents' home. She accused me of rejecting her! I decided I didn't want to go home yet and would stay here for now. I got the bus to my school in the mornings and received regular pocket money. I didn't have any decent clothes and was still wearing mums pass me down bras so I was taken shopping for necessities. Mum complained about what they were doing regarding the clothes and pocket money and she wanted me to change to a different school in case I spread any rumours about that she had thrown me out.

I had been there a few weeks when the Foster Parents had a go at me. They asked me why I hadn't brought any of my personal belongings and made their house feel more like home. I hadn't just in case I went home at some point and would have to move it all back again. I felt under pressure from them and went to Mum's house for my record player, hair things and ornaments. It did make me feel more at home but then Mum had a go at me saying that I had emptied my room and "How could you?" – I couldn't win!

In November Mum was admitted to hospital again briefly and Tracey was placed at, Wimbrick Hey. At least I couldn't get the blame this time as I wasn't at home to make her ill! We visited Mum in the hospital and I stupidly told her of how I'd been on the bus going to school one morning and I'd had an egg fight with one of the boys. I suppose it was my way of getting some attention by showing off to her. The boy had got me the day before so I decided to get him back. The only problem was when I threw my egg on the top deck of the bus to school, he ducked and it completely missed him hitting an unsuspecting passenger on the back of the head instead.

She jumped up and screamed at me "You stupid little bitch!"

I was horrified at what I'd done but at the same time I couldn't contain my laughter. I was in big trouble now. I offered to pay for the cleaning of her coat but the lady complained to the school. I don't blame her of course, I shouldn't have done it. Mum said she didn't want to see me ever again as my news had upset her too much.

Christmas soon came and I spent the day with my new foster family. I came down the stairs in the morning with my foster sister to a chair full of presents. I received a black pencil skirt and a cerise pink jumper, umbrella and a new ski coat. My foster sister Sue and I looked the business. We went for a walk around the estate to strut our stuff. We also both got a whip and top each.

My first thought was "What the hell are they?" but Matt showed us how to use them and we had such a laugh whipping and spinning them. They were lots of fun. Sue and I would go out in the evenings with her ghetto blaster and listen to Madonna songs. We had a laugh sometimes but I felt quite intimidated by her. She always took the lead and was quite bolshie. I just went along with it, not wanting to cause any trouble.

Mum phoned Brenda and Matt one day over the Christmas weekend demanding that I was to go home. I was supposed to have gone for a day but George had made a mistake and told me not to. He'd assumed Mum didn't want me to go again after the egg thing. Well, she had said she didn't want to see me again!! Matt wasn't happy with Mum's attitude and told her she would have to speak to George. I was very confused and upset by the whole thing.

I visited home once a week after Christmas. Mum and I still had the occasional row. One of these rows resulted in her telling me to go and never come back again. I remember waiting outside the house for a bit and then trying to go back in and apologise but I got nowhere. She refused to let me in. I was making an effort but Mum wasn't playing ball. In the whole eleven months I stayed with my Foster Parents, Mum did not visit me once. She complained of not having the bus fare to visit me despite buying herself and Tracey brand new trainers.

On the 27th January a meeting was held. It was an excellent meeting and it was agreed I would stay with my Foster Parents longer than was originally thought. I wasn't ready to go home yet and I felt quite relieved. The next day, to my surprise, Mum phoned me and said the meeting had only been held to put her down and she could not envisage me coming home ever! I was devastated. Matt walked in to find me sobbing and took the phone from me mid conversation. Mum accused him of saying she was a useless parent. She accused both Brenda and Matt of attacking her and making her feel completely inadequate and run down. He put the phone down after telling her not to phone again in that state as it was upsetting for me. George agreed with him that he had done the right thing. Mum was never happy with my Foster Parents again after that. Matt was the first person ever to stick up for me like that.

I sensed the bad feeling between Mum and my Foster Parents and I played on it. I passed comments that had been made back and forth. I thought that if Mum didn't like them she would have me back home, but no, I just got myself in to trouble again for elaborating things that *had* been said. I did exaggerate I admit.

I got fed up living with my Foster Parents as I felt that I was getting picked on despite the fact that Matt had defended me that one time. I had several tantrums over the next few months and one good hiding. Apart from the hiding Matt was OK but Brenda could be quite abrupt and offhand. She complained that I was lazy but I didn't really know what was expected of me. I must have just come across that way. At home I'd done cooking, cleaning and shopping so why would I not want to help here? She criticised the way I wore my hair. Sue started bullying me too and I couldn't say anything because I knew they would side with her, she was their daughter so I just put up with her nasty comments and bullying. I was accused of shoplifting once when in fact it was her that had persuaded me to do it with her bully boy tactics. I'd never have done it on my own. Mum then cancelled another of my visits when she found out about it.

Matt was part of an American football team and one of the fellow players' girlfriends was a dancer. She was very pretty and was a beauty advisor. In the spring she set up a cheerleading group. Sue and I were to be cheerleaders with a few of her friends. We were kitted out in black ski pants and white tops and went to the park to practice the dances and songs with the other girls. We went to the away matches and had a lot of fun. I had the biggest mouth and bellowed across the field "We're the wolves and we're coming after you, singing doo-wah didee didee-dum didee doo!" It was great! Between times though I was unhappy and I asked to be moved. I was told no. I was going to stay there as a punishment for my behaviour and that it was no wonder my Mum didn't like me.

From June to August things went well. My school praised me (which they mostly did) and no one complained about me. Even in light of this, Mum still went on holiday with Tracey and left me behind. It didn't really bother me at the time but it was still a mean thing to do. Things eventually came to a head.

One afternoon in September Brenda and Matt's nineteen year old son came in to the kitchen and said to me, "Make us a cheese butty, please?" He was a big lad and quite intimidating so I hurriedly set about the kitchen.

Sue waltzed in looked at me and said, "Hadn't you better ask me Mum first?"

I felt stupid; he was nineteen, why should I have to ask to make *him* a sandwich? I kept my mouth shut and stood there like a lemon not knowing what to do. She repeated the question nastily. I huffed and walked past her to go and ask Brenda is it OK if I make a sandwich, when Sue punched me full force in the middle of my back knocking me forwards. That was **IT.**

Eleven months of rage boiled over. I'd been bullied, poked, taunted, intimidated, listened to her telling me how she was the cock of her school and getting me in to trouble for shop lifting. I'd had Mum cancelling visits for crap reasons and that was it. I turned around and swung at her, then got hold of her by her hair and dragged her from one end of the room to the other, ending by the bottom of the stairs. I laid in to her punching her in the back. It all happened so quickly. Brenda came flying out by which time Sue was on the floor. She wouldn't bully me again.

Brenda picked up the handful of hair I'd ripped out of Sue's head and said, "Sue had alopecia when she was a baby" and she swung for me and slapped me hard across the face.

I didn't know!!! At that point Matt came running in from out side.

"What are you doing?" he shouted.

He went on to say how Sue had been picking on me for some months now and it was about time I stuck up for myself.

Hallelujah! Someone had seen what she had been doing! But a row erupted between them. I couldn't cope. Everywhere I went I caused trouble. Now they were going to get divorced all because of me. Well that's what I thought anyway. I didn't want to stay there a minute longer.

I retreated into my shell after that. Brenda was awful to me. This was exactly what I had predicted. That they would stick up for their own. Sue was her daughter and I was just some emotionally disturbed rebel with no attachment to her.

Brenda was having a go at me the day after I'd laid in to Sue and I didn't know if I was coming or going.

First she said, "Go to your room!"

Then it was, "Stay where you are!"

Then when her friend arrived, "Go to your room!" again so I was out of the way.

It was like she wanted me to flip my box. I ran up the stairs to the bedroom screaming in frustration and swept my arm across the top of the chest of drawers knocking everything on to the floor and flumped on to the bed.

Brenda came bounding up behind me and shouted, *"Here, let me help you!"* and she proceeded to smash my room up throwing my things everywhere. All my belongings crashed to the floor and then I watched in horror as two of the three frogs I had won at primary school shattered into pieces.

She told a different story saying I had head butted her in the face nearly knocking her out, kicked the back of her ankles and I had wrecked the bedroom. I really don't know why she lied and of course she would be believed - not me.

On the 11th September 1986 I was moved to Wimbrick Hey Assessment Centre.

10. Wimbrick Hey

At last, somewhere I could be me. No one looked down on me here or blamed me for things I hadn't done. All the staff were lovely and they didn't find fault with me at all. They all had funny nicknames here rather than being aunties and uncles.

My room was a bit like a prison cell, all plain pale green and just a cupboard and chest of drawers but that didn't really matter. I settled in well. No complaints were made about me and I was happy. I met my best friend Debbie here. She bounded into one of the upstairs lounges one afternoon and continued to jog on the spot while waiting to speak to a member of staff. I thought she was a boy at first. She had short dark hair, was very tall for her age and wore glasses. We hit it off straight away. We were like chalk and cheese, but we became best friends.

At Wimbrick we were taken swimming regularly, got pocket money, dyed our hair and shared household jobs just like you would at home. We weren't allowed out on our own as it was an assessment centre but there was plenty to do, with a snooker table and a mountain of cushions here to watch the telly too!

I stayed here for two months and if I'd had my way I would have stayed there forever. Unfortunately it was a short term care home only. Debbie and I were very well behaved and we went everywhere together. We two were the first ever children to be let out from Wimbrick Hey without supervision due to our good attitudes. We were so proud of ourselves. We went shopping in Moreton Cross and went to the fair in New Brighton at the weekends. One of the other girls came to the fair with us the first time we went and persuaded me to go on the waltzers and the gravity wheel. I was so scared to go on the gravity wheel, but I did it and loved it. I'd never been to the fair before and I had the time of my life.

At bedtimes we had a laugh too. There was always supper in the communal dining room of crumpets or eggs and toast then off to bed. One night after lights out I came out of my bedroom to go to the loo which was directly opposite. When I came back out of the toilet I went in to Debbie's room instead of mine which was next door to my bedroom. The corridors were wings like a prison, and a member of staff would sit at the bottom on night duty. I didn't think they'd notice being right the way down at the bottom and all the rooms looking exactly the same, but they soon did. They saw the funny side of it though and sent me back to my bedroom. It wasn't an issue.

On Halloween night we all got dressed up in black bin bags and had a party. There was going to be a special supper and later on we were all sent down to the dining area. We made our way there but it seemed very quiet. The lights had been switched off when we got to the dining room in an effort to be spooky and we stopped dead in our tracks. All of a sudden staff came from everywhere out of the darkness with buckets of water hurling them at us. The lights came on and it was the biggest water fight you have ever seen. We were drenched and we roared with laughter. The floor was an inch high flood. Such fun!

That night, after drying off, I stood on my radiator and stuck my head out of the tiny bedroom window and Debbie next door did the same. We could pass ciggies to each other in our stretched out witches hats as they reached further than your arm did. If that failed we used a bristle hair brush and wedged the cigarette in the bristles.

Other times we had spit races down the wall. Disgustingly funny! One time I got my head stuck when a member of staff was walking below. I pulled my ciggie in and wrestled with the small window. I howled with laughter as I tried to pull my jammed head in.

I used to get the bus to school from Wimbrick when I had gone back for the autumn term. It was a bit of a journey every morning but I was glad that I had not been moved to a different school. One day, I met a nice boy on the bus, who was going to work. He was only sixteen and on a training scheme not far from my school. We got on really well and decided to go out together on a date. I remember meeting him one day in Morton cross. I saw him from way over the roundabout on the other side of the road. He looked like an angel. His hair shone in the autumn sun and gleamed gold like a halo. He was beautiful. He took me to New Brighton for the day. We started going out together. I would come in from school late in the week with a huge smile on my face and my tie half way round my neck. The girls laughed at me. They knew id been kissing him on the way home.

We weren't together for very long. He said he was still grieving for a girlfriend that had died in an accident a few months before. He had both halves of a key ring that fitted together to make one and claimed the second one was hers and that she was six foot under. I naively didn't know what that meant and asked him. He told me he was dying too and gave that as his excuse for finishing our brief relationship. I know it sounds far fetched but at my age I believed him. I broke my heart and ended up breaking down and crying at the swimming baths that evening. I told one of the girls from the home when she asked me what was wrong and she hugged me affectionately.

I have never seen him since and often wonder whether *maybe* he was telling the truth. I'll never know. He looked like an angel so maybe God wanted him back.

Things were worse with my Mum now than ever. Several weekend visits were cancelled again as she said she couldn't afford it. One row too many over something pointless and trivial was the turning point for me. I'd spat in the bath at home and Mum had overreacted. That was the moment I chose not to ever go home again. I decided for myself that I would go to Parkside Children's Home to live permanently. I couldn't stay at Wimbrick Hey so I had to go somewhere! At fourteen, even I knew I needed stability and I would never get that at home.

On 15th November 1986 I was transferred to Parkside Children's Home, my new home.

11. Parkside (My Home)

It was daunting moving to Parkside. It was a much bigger home and some of the children here were quite intimidating, some of them downright bullies. I had been here once before for the Christmas disco they held annually for all the care homes. The Christmas tree was huge and reached at least twenty feet up into a part of the building that didn't have an upstairs bit. Parkside was an L shaped building the same as Wimbrick Hey; with one wing all dining and communal areas, and an office and a huge kitchen on the ground floor. The kitchen had two cooks who worked alternate days. The upstairs had three flats and one bedroom. The other wing was bedrooms top and bottom with a small TV room on the bottom.

This was my new home! There were rules and regulations, the same as anywhere. I got pocket money, went to town on the bus and thankfully stayed at the same school. I loved my school.

My first few days were awful. I was the new girl so I was a target for the bullies. On my first day I was bullied by two sisters, Katy and Kara, and another girl who I knew by sight from Wimbrick, who thought she was Madonna. I later found out Kara had a reputation for this kind of thing.

On my first night there they were just name-calling

Parkside (My Home)

and being nasty to me and they backed me into a corner. Kara had a wet flannel and was slapping me with it. I wouldn't fight back. There were three of them and one of me. She ended up throwing it at me so I grabbed at it and threw it back in her face and ran. They chased me around the building for retaliating but the staff told them to leave me alone when they saw what was happening. I was left alone after that. Maybe they were testing me to see if I could stand up for myself.

My bedroom had three beds, but in the room were just Katy and me. On my first night, she sang out loudly in unison with her friend in the next room, keeping me awake.

Katy did say to me, *"We're just havin' a laugh, you'll get used to it,"* and I thought maybe she'd be OK with me after all.

I felt so lonely and curled up in my bed and cried myself to sleep. I awoke the next morning and Katy was gone. Her mattress was off the bed and turned up long ways against the wall with no sheets on it. It was all stained. I later found out that she and the girl from Wimbrick Hey had overdosed on iron tablets and had been taken to hospital in the middle of the night. I hadn't heard a thing. The girl from Wimbrick didn't come back to Parkside again and when Katy came back she went into a different bedroom.

The next couple of nights were subject to the fire brigade arriving, all sirens and lights a-blazing. A few of the girls used to sneak up in the night and spray the smoke detectors with hairspray or light a match under them, which set them off. There was a direct link to the fire brigade and so they were called out every time. I never actually did it but watched the other girls do it and thought it was funny at the time. Understandably, the staff were furious and everyone was grounded.

It was a month before Christmas and things were still bad between Mum and me. She took to complaining to the school about me and accusing George of doing nothing to help. There were arguments over food, money, smoking and Christmas presents. She threatened to not have me home over Christmas. A few days later she said she didn't want me home that week either.

After another visit later in December, Mum accused me of making her ill again and causing her depression. (Mum was ill long before I was on the scene). This was the straw that broke the camels back. I decided to stay at Parkside on my own. *I* was ill. Ill with being let down!! All the other kids went home for Christmas and I stayed at Parkside by myself. I was the only child not to go home for Christmas. On Christmas Eve George came to see me with a gift. He wondered if I had changed my mind about going home but I hadn't. Enough was enough.

On Christmas Day, I had a lovely surprise, courtesy of George. My best mate Debbie from Wimbrick bounced her bubbly self in and we hugged each other. George had arranged it for us to spend Christmas together, bless him. Debbie told me how she'd cried out of her window when I had left and her mission in life was to get moved to Parkside to be with me.

When she eventually moved in we were inseparable. We shared our bedroom and made it our own, putting posters up. I visited her family. We went to the pictures together and saw *Dirty Dancing*, still one of my favourite films, and *Hellraiser*. We were so scared watching Hellraiser that we smoked twenty cigarettes one after the other. We listened to Queen records and banged on the windows of the upstairs corridor in unison to *We Will Rock You* and *You're My Best Friend*, which became our song. We walked to the bus stop together in the morning even though we went to different schools and we even made sure our dentist appointments synchronised. That way we could make a day of it and didn't get in to trouble! One day we jumped up and down and rolled around in puddles so we were soaking wet and had to go back home. We told the staff we'd been caught in the rain and got soaked by a passing bus and would have to stay off school. They weren't daft: they sent us to school after we dried ourselves off. We got up to all kinds and had a scream together. She made my life worth living.

It was around this time I met my new boyfriend, Mark. I was ready for bed one night and had on my mint green fleecy sleep suit, rather like a giant Telly tubby. I had got a bit lost in the building as I'd only been there a few weeks and it was huge. I wandered in through an open door to a sitting area and plonked myself down on the sofa. A youngish man was there talking to another lad.

"Oh, I didn't know this room was here," I said, and then I asked the man "Are you one of the staff?"

He laughed and said "Well, you could say that, yes."

I assumed he was one of the staff and carried on watching his TV and chatting to him. Eventually I realised he wasn't staff at all; he lived there as a resident and this was his flat. I apologised and got up to go, very embarrassed.

He said, "No, don't go, its OK. Some of the other girls come in sometimes to sing and dance. It's fine." I came to see him regularly after that. I was relaxed and no staff bothered me there.

Mark wasn't much to look at. He had long red hair, was a bit freckly and had huge ears. He was nice enough to begin with and I got on well with him. He was sixteen and had been in care all of his life. It wasn't long before we were going out together.

In January 1987, Mum was in hospital again. I visited, taking Debbie along with me. Debbie and I were messing about, I have to confess. We were just being silly and egging each other on. It was nothing drastic, just making silly noises, giggling and daft faces. I probably did embarrass Mum with my silliness. She didn't want to see me again after that and tried to get me moved to another home that was stricter. **Stricter?** What did she want? Prison?

Getting caught smoking outside school didn't help matters too much either.

In February, my meetings with Mark were discovered and a contract was put in place over where and when I could see him. I just saw it as everyone having a go at me again, trying to control me. I was still in the building so I didn't see what the problem was. It seemed that every time I found a bit of happiness someone tried to take it away from me. I broke that contract by being in Mark's flat when I shouldn't have been, and was consequently banned from it for three days. I started being aggressive

Parkside (My Home)

at school now due to my feelings of inferiority and got myself sent home for 'throwing a wobbler'. The deputy head teacher, who I think loved me to bits, understood why I was frustrated and said she was sending me home to give me some much needed space.

In March, I decided I was going to find my Dad. Mum didn't want to know me so I'd go and find him. I had an address for him but George said to hang on until he had written to him first. He discussed the possibility of him not wanting to see me and said it was best that he made contact first.

I hadn't visited Mum for three months at home now and refused to visit in the future taking my record player and other things to Parkside. It had been a recommendation at one of my review meetings that Mum should visit me once a week but this never happened. She accused the staff of *'being against her'* and *'siding with me'* and couldn't face them. She accused me of taking things from her home when I'd gone for my record player and *'what else I had taken.'* I hadn't taken anything! Tracey had lent me her coat and she'd hit the roof, passing a message on to the home for me to take it back.

That was it. I couldn't wait for George to write to my Dad any longer. I was going to see my Dad as soon as possible. I decided to go to the address I had. Mark and his best friend came with me for support. I was a bag of nerves. What if he didn't live there anymore or he didn't want to know me?

I went to the address that I'd got from Mum a long while ago on the bus. It was a high-rise block of flats in Birkenhead and it was right on the top floor. We got in the lift which stank of wee and made our way up. *This was it!*

I knocked on the door and a man answered. He had smiley eyes and a moustache. I started to stutter not knowing how to word what I was about to say. I knew it would be a shock. After all it had been ten years. I proceeded to tell him my name and who I was and that this was the address that my mother had given to me.

He just looked bewildered and said "No, no, he doesn't live here anymore. Must have moved out. It's a sad case."

I wasn't sure whether to believe him or not. There was something in his manner that I just couldn't put my finger on. A twinkle in his eyes.

He repeated, "Oh no, it's a sad case, a sad case."

He was quite funny and made us laugh but I went away disappointed and bemused.

It turned out he really was my Dad. I'd totally blown him away by turning up on his door step so he'd denied it, in a panic. He contacted George a few days later. He had got George's number from the letter he received from him, after my surprise visit. He decided he wanted to see us. George was a bit upset that I hadn't waited but I think he understood. He persuaded me to see Mum on the way home for five minutes. I agreed and he picked me up from school and took me there. For once we had a civil conversation and on my way home I said to George "I wish my Mum could be like that all the time."

Mum came for tea at Parkside that week and it all

went very well. Two weeks later Tracey and I went to see Dad together. It was awkward at first but we soon got chatting. He went on his CB and was telling all his friends he had his two daughters with him. He sounded really proud. Mum had even made a fruit cake for us to take to him. "Has it got arsenic in it?" He joked. When we left he gave us a big hug and a kiss.

In May, Parkside's annual holiday was coming up. Every year in May we went to Pontin's for a weekend and we had two weeks at camp later on in the year. I kicked off because I didn't want to go and was told I had no choice. I had become extremely obsessed with my boyfriend Mark and could not bear to be away from him. I had been seeing him for a about five months now and had started sleeping with him. I knew sex before marriage was wrong and I should have waited, but I loved him. I was living in cloud cuckoo land. I thought we would be together forever, get married and live happily ever after, so it wouldn't matter if I slept with him now anyway.

I was so wrong. We started arguing because I was so possessive and he was so selfish. I wanted to be with him all the time. We just got sick of each other but I didn't want to admit it. He started ignoring me and locking me out of his flat all the time. I would hammer on his door and scream at him to let me in. I couldn't believe it. I had given my self to him and now he was shutting me out. I became really depressed and this caused problems for me at school.

One day I ran out of a lesson and bolted down the road. I can't remember why. My form tutor came after me in her car. I hid in a bush in someone's garden and watched her sail past. I didn't bank on her sailing past again the other direction and when I stepped out of the bushes she spotted me. She stopped me and took me back to school.

George took us to see our Dad again on the 20th May 1987. It was great. He played video games with us and lent me two of his Queen cassettes. "Brilliant", I thought," He likes Queen too!"

He asked George about taking us out to Southport for the day, and to see some relatives on his side of the family. When Mum found out about it she wasn't happy stating that Dad was a crazy driver and probably had no tax or insurance. That was ten years ago!

Nevertheless arrangements were to be made on my return from my holiday at Pontin's.

12. Camp

I stayed in a chalet with Debbie and a member of staff, Mary, on our weekend away. Mary was my Key Worker. Everyone had a specific key worker allocated to them in Parkside so that you had one member of staff that you could go and talk to if you felt the need. Mary was mine and she was fantastic. She was like a Mum to me. She had her own family and children too but I could tell she loved me very much.

She said to me a few times "You remind me of myself when I was your age."

I think that's why I could relate to her and she could relate to me.

I played in the adventure park for most of the holiday and wandered around the site. I was a bit bored to be honest because all the other kids had gone off somewhere and I had no idea what to do with myself. We had only been at the site for a few hours when one of the chalets some of the other kids were staying in was burgled. All the money had been taken for the whole weekend's food and entertainment. The boss from Parkside was most upset and had to go all the way back to the home to get more money.

On our first day Mary was making our meal. It was Fray Bentos pies in their tins. I got really excited. Dad used to eat Fray Bentos pies out of the tin, Mum had told me. I was going to eat mine out of the tin, just like my Dad!

I said, "I'm OK thanks, I don't need a plate."

Mary said, "You're not eating out of the tin,"

"I want it out of the tin, that's how my Dad used to have them."

"I don't care what your Dad did; you'll have a plate like everyone else!"

We had an argument and I lost the plot over *a pie in a tin?*

In the evenings we went in to the on-site show bar with the staff. There was a competition on one night and Debbie and I had been practising our dance routine all day so we could enter. We were nervous but we did it. The staff took photos of us. We didn't win but at least we'd had a go. The other kids were all still somewhere else. It turned out they were all in the sites other late night club. There was a rumour spreading that it was Uncle Kev from Edge Hill that had stolen the money and had taken all the other girls out clubbing. I wouldn't know personally but it did look a bit suspect to me.

I was fifteen in June and only had another year of school left now. I didn't have a clue what I wanted to do. I had chosen my options the year before and my subjects were Child Care, Art, Home Economics Commerce and French. I was extremely good at art. Mum had always said I could be a famous designer. I used to pick up old Barbie dolls from jumble sales and make Victorian and

Elizabethan costumes for them out of bits of lace and material. I sat for hours sewing. They were very good.

I'd had a try on the potter's wheel as part of an art lesson once too and had produced on my first attempt, *a perfect pot*. I had turned the wheel gently with my foot against the pedal keeping it in control. I kept my hands in a still position and caressed the clay as it ran through my hands, then added some more water and gently moulded it to a curved pot. The teacher thought it was a fluke and invited me to try again. I produced another perfect pot. She was most impressed, asking had I done it before and said she had never seen a pot like it on a first attempt. She mentioned taking it up as a profession but nothing ever came of her suggestion. I don't know why as I would have loved to have done it.

I was also very interested in cooking. I enjoyed that, but I hated commerce and just messed about in lessons out of sheer boredom. French was becoming tiresome too. I had achieved one hundred percent in my mock exams last year and was fluent with a good accent. I was one of only five in the year to gain this result so was automatically put on the option. The only problem was I was in one of the lower forms and possibly a bit slower than the other girls who were in the top two forms in the year. I couldn't keep up with them. I was embarrassed. One day I decided to bunk off in the fifth year toilets. I had a smoke and sat off on my own. The teacher came looking for me on noticing my absence and found me in there.

She asked me, "What are you doing in here?"

I coolly answered, "I'm bunking your French lesson!"

One thing I'm not is a liar, I am proud to say.

Yet again in July a mix up with visiting arrangements to see Dad left me irate. Tracey had started staying over at Parkside now and again and we got to spend some time together. We had always been kept apart and never developed a proper relationship together. She had also started at my school as she had caught up academically. I was really pleased to be spending time with her and felt very protective towards her.

We went shopping one day and she bought a skirt. Unfortunately it didn't fit her. I offered to swap it with one of mine and she agreed, to save her taking it back. I was just trying to help. Big mistake. I swear the subject wasn't dropped for at least three weeks. I was told to pay Tracey for the skirt. I had my pocket money stopped. Mum cancelled another visit because of it and it caused no end of problems.

I started getting pressure over the visits to Dad too. Everything seemed to revolve around Tracey and when it was convenient for her, causing more resentment between us. I had just had three weeks of grief over a skirt and now I was to fall in to place with her plans. I wasn't having it and told them so in colourful language.

I went to see my Dad, on my own, on the bus. He was really pleased to see me and couldn't wait to show me off to his friends. As we set out, Dad made a point of taking my hand and holding it as we walked down the road to our destination. I was fifteen now and, not uncomfortable but aware I probably looked a bit stupid at my age holding hands with your Dad. I wanted to hold his hand though and kept my grip. I saw this as a clear indication that he was sorry for the time he hadn't let me hold my Mum's hand at Bidston Hill. It was a little moment between me and him. I didn't know it at the time but this would be the last time I saw my Dad for over 20 years.

In August it was time for our two week camping trip. I had to leave Mark for an excruciating whole two weeks. I stayed at Abbey Crus in a tent with Debbie. I hated the showers; they were minging and full of creepy-crawlies. There was a stream at the back of the camp site which was fun. We hitched our pants up and paddled in it. The rocks hurt your feet but it was good fun. Walks around the abbey on the site were interesting too, provoking discussion of the Headless Monk. I climbed the big hills and went for midnight rambles with the staff. I climbed up the Back Hill, as it was called and earned myself an extra pound pocket money. I ripped my leg open though, climbing over a stile!. The scar on my knee is a fond permanent reminder of it. I remember reaching the top of one hill on an evening trek and lay on the ground gazing up at the stars. It was lovely and so peaceful. When we came down the hill we slid most of the way on our bottoms in the sheep poo. We got our pocket money while we were there rationed out daily. Two pounds a day for sweets or ice cream or souvenirs. Sadly I went without ice cream and sweets and saved like a trooper to buy Mark a ring. What a pleb!!

The Horseshoe Falls were near by the camp site. A huge lake with a horse shoe shape water fall and surrounding fields was to be our picnic spot. We spent the day there. A rope swing had been hung in one of the huge trees at the edge of the lake that swung you out over the silver ripples. I threw myself in to the water and swam to the other side of the lake. I was quite pleased with myself. Picnicking there was fun. I was fascinated watching the jam and the sardine sandwiches being made. Even more fascinated when a young boy who was with us was eating one of them. He breathed in, opened his mouth to take a bite and promptly swallowed a bee. He nearly choked to death!

Back at Parkside after camp it was time for another review. Prior to my review, discussions had taken place without my knowledge about whether or not I was sexually active with Mark and whether I should be put on the pill. Mum had point blank refused to let me go on the pill, saying that it would be a *'free license.'*

It's a shame no one asked me what *I* wanted to do at this second meeting. They just stopped me seeing him as much thinking that would work. I had to stay in for two more nights of the week. It only caused more bad feeling on my behalf and led me to run from the room hurling abuse at, Mrs A, the boss of Parkside.

In September there was another mix up with arrangements for visiting Mum. She sent a nasty letter to poor George complaining about it. Arrangements for visiting Dad on the other hand were to be fortnightly, pleasing Tracey and I.

The next month was a collection of problems one after the other. I would occasionally go to Mum's from school at lunch time, as Mum's house was ten minutes down the road. I thought it would be nice to spend half an hour with her. I would ask if it was OK to make a sandwich for my lunch and she agreed. I thought we were getting on well until she complained to George again that I was going and eating all her food. She could not afford to feed me and George was to pass on a message telling me not to go at lunch times anymore. Another favourite of Mums was my turning up unannounced. That wasn't allowed either.

"You'll have to make an appointment and go through the correct channels," I think that was her words.

My life was full of reviews, appointments, meetings, tension and not enough understanding. Any snippets of love from Mary were snatched at and I didn't see my beloved Aunty Jane any more; being in care put a stop to that. Before I had received the message not to go home at lunch times anymore I had turned up unannounced again, completely oblivious to any problem. Mum started having a go at me about it and I couldn't understand what I'd done wrong this time.

A few days later Tracey and I had a huge fight at home. I think it was about the fact that she was smoking and getting in to trouble, yet she hadn't been stuck in care like me. I didn't think it was fair. It resulted in my walking out and saying I wouldn't go to our Dad's with her that night. According to Mum, we wrecked the kitchen.

A member of staff told me off when I got back to Parkside. I was made to stay in another night after rowing about it even though I'd already done my two nights in. I got in to trouble again a few days later. I had asked Mrs A for some socks as all of mine were either missing or stolen. A simple request. If socks weren't nailed down you didn't see them again. She refused, saying I must have mislaid them and It was my fault for being careless. She just thought I was being manipulative. I explained I had put them in the wash and not got them back, which was a regular occurrence, but she was not interested. I went to school in my stiletto heels that morning as my buckskin creepers rubbed my feet with no socks on. I went straight to my deputy head and explained this to her. She was very sympathetic and impressed with my attitude and the fact I had gone straight to her with my problem. I don't know what she said to Mrs A, but when I got home that night after school there were five pairs of white socks on my bed. I believe I was triumphant!

A similar thing happened when my school shoes were wrecked. The sole had come off at the front and I was made to glue them instead of getting a new pair. OK fair enough! The problem was that the sole came off again and I tripped up nearly breaking my neck. Gluing them was clearly not going to work. I took them to the office and showed them to Mrs A. I couldn't wear them like that anymore. I was quite civil until she refused again to let me get another pair and told me to glue the damaged ones again.

I screamed at her. "I've glued them once, I can't glue them again!"

I flung the shoes straight at her in foul temper. She *hated* me!

I believe Mrs A really did hate me. I remember being quite ill at some point with a chest infection. I desperately needed my Ventolin inhaler but she had taken it off me. I told her I was desperate for it but she cruelly refused to give it to me locking it away in the office. As I was a smoker she didn't think I should have it. In principle, she had a point but I was genuinely ill. I started to hyper ventilate and I really couldn't breathe. I was light-headed and had to tilt my head backwards to open up my airways in a desperate attempt to get some air in. I was extremely lucky that a boy in the home just so happened to have an inhaler as he was also asthmatic and he rushed to get it for me. I think he may have saved me a trip to the hospital!

After my fight at home I refused to see Mum and she refused to see me until I apologised. George suggested to Mum: "Gina's whole behaviour appears to centre around jealousy and the need for attention." That's exactly what was wrong with me. He had hit the nail on the head. How sad nothing ever came of it.

That October, I had a big fight with Mark. Our relationship was really bad and we fought a lot. I constantly tested him to see if he loved me. I wound him up and he always retaliated by hitting me. After one fight I locked myself in the toilet for half an hour.

Another meeting took place on 15th October. I had no intention of going to it to be pulled apart as usual. I conveniently disappeared when everyone else arrived. I was grounded for not going to it. Mum then requested another meeting in the run up to Christmas. Again I thought I couldn't cope with yet another meeting. It was like everyone was on at me all the time, which just made me feel more and more hatred inside. I was frustrated at school, had been disruptive and taken out of class. I was suspended for two weeks after losing my temper with the teachers.

The meeting went ahead on 16th November and the Christmas arrangements were made without my presence. I didn't care. It was around this time I got really ill. I couldn't eat. The sight of greasy food made me heave. I was tired and sick.

The reason for my frustration of late…...

I was pregnant!

13. Pregnant!

I didn't realize I could be pregnant until I was complaining of feeling ill one day in the corridor near the staff office. I had been using the so-called Safe method which turned out to be not that safe for me.

A quite loud member of staff asked "Do you think you could be pregnant?"

I immediately said, "No" and insisted I was still a virgin.

She asked me again. "Are you sure?"

I couldn't say anything. There were people everywhere and I was embarrassed. I didn't want anyone to know I was having sex because then Mum would find out and I'd just get in to trouble again. I wish she had taken me aside and asked me. I think she must have told Mary what she thought, as Mary asked me later on, in private. I still tried to deny it to her saying I was still a virgin. She wasn't daft. I did a pregnancy test.

A couple of days later I was called to the office to see Mrs A. My head had been chocker for days thinking "Was I? Wasn't I?" I had sat and ate my meal, picking the batter off a crispy fish and I couldn't even entertain the chips a week before. I went in to the office and sat myself down.

Straight to the point Mrs A said, "Right, what are you going to do then?"

I looked at her blankly.

"Well, I've made an appointment for you at the clinic to see about an abortion."

Again, I looked at her blank thinking 'You're jumping the gun a bit, aren't you?'

"I need to get my test result back first, so I don't know yet."

"Well, yes you are."

I looked at her. "Are what? I haven't had the result yet, I don't know if I am or not."

She said, "You *are* pregnant. I've got the result here."

I burst in to tears. All I could think was 'I'm pregnant, I'm pregnant!'

I think it was atrocious the way I was told. Yes, I'd been mighty stupid but I didn't deserve that. An appointment for the clinic had been made for an abortion before I even new the results of my test. I felt I had no choice but to go through with it.

It was like everything else, you do as you're told or you will get in trouble. Change your attitude or I don't want to see you anymore.

At the clinic for my pre-op I felt like everyone was disgusted with me. I had degraded and hated myself. I wouldn't mind, I didn't even believe in sex before marriage, I was a Christian and here I was. Stupid me. I remember

Pregnant!

the doctor sternly saying I needed three signatures to go ahead and asking what was I going to do in the future as he didn't want to see me again.

I didn't want to see him again either. It wasn't my choice to be there in the first place. I said nothing; I'd only get in to trouble. George's impression was that I would have kept the baby had I had more support from Parkside. Maybe! I'll never know now.

I told Mark the news. He just looked at me vacantly and said nothing. No opinions, no words of comfort or anything, just a blank expression. And that was it. He just left me to get on with it.

My appointment for the termination was made for between Christmas and New Year. Mark decided he wasn't going with me as he was going to Southport for Christmas with his best friend. I was distraught. He was going off to have a great time instead of supporting me. He was leaving me to go and get rid of my baby at Christmas on my own. I was hysterical shouting and crying, pleading with him not to go. How could he?

At this point, my best friend Debbie didn't know that I was pregnant and thought I was out of order for spoiling Mark's fun. She had a bit of a go at me because she didn't understand the situation. I argued with her trying to hold the truth back. She continued to side with Mark going away. It was Christmas and he should be allowed to go off with his mate if he wanted to.

I blurted it out to her. "I'm pregnant!"

Her face fell and she understood. Realisation dawned.

When Mum found out she cancelled all the Christmas visits. She didn't want to see me and was worried everyone would blame her for not letting me go on the pill. She had to go to the hospital to sign the documents but she wouldn't come near me even then. After all that she still refused to let me take the pill, which Mrs A strongly objected to. She was more interested in pressing charges against Mark for statutory rape which caused yet another argument.

On Christmas day I was the only child in Parkside. Again. I woke up to all my presents at the bottom of the bed, which I knew Mary had been shopping for. All the residents got an allotted amount of money for clothes and separate money for whatever we wanted to buy in Parkside but these presents were extra. I spent the day on my own.

In the last few days of December, I was taken to the hospital and dropped off. I felt ashamed and guilty. I could feel all eyes on me and I know what I must have looked like. All I had for comfort was my ghetto blaster and some ear phones. There were pregnant mums trying to keep their babies and other women who had lost theirs. I stayed there on my own and had my termination.

14. Not so Sweet Sixteen

After Tracey had started at my school she had confided in me about something. I can't remember exactly when it was but I know how honoured I felt that she came to speak to me. It must have been before I had been pregnant as after that I wasn't really qualified to dish out advice. She was only just thirteen and she had thought she was pregnant. I didn't even know she had a boyfriend. He was eighteen, a lot older than her. I know I was too young to be in that kind of relationship and she was even younger than me! I was worried for her and told her to get a pregnancy test. If she wasn't pregnant she didn't need to say anything to Mum. If she was too scared to ask to go on the pill she could use the safe method as I had (of course that turned out to be not so safe in my case).

For a month after my termination I couldn't even look at George. He tried to talk to me a few times but I would walk away, too ashamed. I liked him but I didn't like myself. Mum was very depressed over it all. I blamed her for what I had gone through for not letting me go on the pill. I was having doubts about my decision too and I felt I'd been pushed in to it. Mark told me he had been against it as well. A bit convenient after the deed was done though. We had a row over it and I was extremely distraught shouting at him,

"I want my baby back!"

He retorted, "Well, go and get it out of the incinerator then!"

I collapsed in a heap at his painful words.

To top that off I received a letter from Mum saying that she thought what I had done was wrong and that there were plenty of couples out there wanting babies who couldn't have children of their own. She said I should have kept the baby and adopted it out. I needed my Mum but all I felt was more anger and disappointment toward me.

My behaviour in school badly deteriorated and their sympathy towards me started to run out. I was always very good at school but recent events just became unbearable.

One of my friends came and took me to one side one day and said "Look, I know it's none of my business, but Linda (the girl id been to camp with when I was thirteen) is telling everyone you've had an abortion."

She didn't press me for information or anything like that; she was just being a mate. I went looking for Linda to tell her to pack it in. I found her and I think I was quite reasonable under the circumstances. I asked her to please not tell anyone else about it, as what I had been through was bad enough without everyone knowing about it. It was a civilised conversation. She agreed and told me that it was my Mum that started the rumour by telling the neighbours. As she was a neighbour's daughter it had got back to her. I couldn't believe it!

An hour later my friend came back and told me, "I'm

really sorry but she's told another three people as far as I'm aware."

"I'm going to effing kill her!" I snapped

I stomped of to search for her. My friend ran off to find her too, to warn her I was going to effing kill her and she managed to get to her before I did. Linda was down one of the corridors and she had her back to me. My friend was hastily warning her of what was to come. She wasn't quick enough though. I tapped Linda on the right shoulder calmly. As she turned round I punched her right on the chin. She spun in the direction my fist had taken her and landed on the floor in a heap.

I screamed at her, "I told you not to tell anyone else! I gave you a chance, I bloody warned you didn't I! Don't do it AGAIN!"

One of the teachers saw the kafuffle and flew down the corridor 'Oh, God, I've had it now!', I thought. To my surprise though, she stopped and asked me if I was alright and took me to the Deputy Head's office. The Deputy Head took me in and sat me down and let me explain to her. She knew what Linda was saying about me and said,

"I don't blame you at all for hitting her. I'd have done the same thing in your shoes."

What a Relief! There was someone who saw it from my point of view. She knew what had happened to me and still had a soft spot for me. She told me not to do it again and I agreed.

Mark's eighteenth birthday was in February. He didn't

really have any family. He never spoke much of them only that they had gone to America with his baby sister and left him behind for some reason. He would be on his own for his special day so I decided to give him a surprise birthday party at his flat. Mark didn't live in his flat at Parkside anymore, he had moved on to his own private flat in town just prior to his coming of age. I visited him whenever I could and still couldn't bear to be without him. I organised the party food, some alcohol, sorted the music out and invited all my friends. There was a good turnout. It was a bit quiet to begin with but the party soon got going. All my friends from school were there and Debbie's sister was there too – she was best friends with another of my friends. Everyone had a good time dancing around the living room and most of us drank far too much. Debbie's sister ended up being sick all over me in the bathroom. I just remember the warm sensation all over my hand. Eeeeee!

At the end of the night nearly everyone had gone home so Mark tried to walk me up the road for a taxi back home. I was in no fit state. I couldn't even walk. He had hold of me under my arms from behind trying to walk me forwards. I panicked that he was going to hit me as it was a regular occurrence so I started screaming. He wouldn't let go of me and I panicked even more. I clenched my fist and punched backwards past my face in to his face behind me. I had to get him off me. He soon let go of me and I then fell backwards cracking the back of my head on a sand stone wall and knocked myself clean out. Everything went black. I couldn't see. Everything was momentarily quiet and still. I felt a cold rush of air down the back of my throat and I suddenly gasped for breath. I had stopped breathing and Mark had given me mouth to mouth. I thought my eyes had been shut the whole time because all I could see was black in front of me. He said they were wide open and staring in to space.

I stayed at his flat that night and slept there. No ambulance was called and no one came to look for me. I woke the next morning to the most horrific headache that lasted for hours, no, days! I made my way back to Parkside to face the music. I explained why I had not made it back home the night before but no one was interested in my injury. I was grounded again. I later found out that whilst I had been asleep at the flat, Mark had had sex with my best friend's sister in the next room.

My next review was due in March. I wasn't looking forward to it. I spoke to George and said I couldn't face my review if the termination was mentioned. I would not go unless he promised me that it wouldn't be. I wanted to forget about it and not feel ashamed. I assumed he had listened to me. The last couple of months I had been doing really well at Parkside, apart from Mark's birthday party. I was keen to concentrate on that. I wrote out my report on how I thought I had been doing with enthusiasm. Mum visited me the day before on my condition that she did not mention the termination either. It actually went really well. I made her a cup of tea in the upstairs lounge and we talked for a while.

The next day arrived and I nervously went into the office. I had never liked any of the meetings or reviews. Not since I was made to sit in a room with a see through mirror to observe my behaviour a few years before. I picked up the report on my seat and sat down to read before the session commenced. The report contained an agenda of things to be discussed at the meeting and comments from staff. I scanned down the page and got to the second paragraph and the words leapt out at me. *Gina's abortion.* A whole paragraph. How *dare* they? I was totally ashamed and deflated. The meeting hadn't even started and I had hoped it would go well. I jumped up and kicked off swearing and shouting. I flew out of the room and up the stairs, ripping the report to shreds as I went. The one thing I'd asked for and I was denied. I didn't see why it had to be discussed. It was over and done with and I didn't want to keep being reminded of what I had done. I had hoped that the discussions would be of my future and not my past. I was hoping to go in to the independent living and move to one of the flats but that didn't look likely now after my outburst.

Mum stayed for the remainder of the meeting and was met with disapproval over the issue of my still not being allowed to go on the pill. She immediately assumed everyone was blaming her for the pregnancy and she got up and left too, saying that she was never coming to Parkside again and she didn't want to see me again, either. I ran out and spoke to her in the car park before she went home and I promised to go and see her. I knew deep down she didn't really mean it.

Tracey hadn't been at my school for very long but she'd latched on to some of my friends, even though they were two years older than she was. She had become very close to one particular friend who was a bit of an attention seeker herself. She had come in to school with sunglasses on one day and told us all she was going blind. This friend, Tina, lived up by my Mum's house and near to the school so she and Tracey started walking home together. Unbeknownst to me they got quite close and Tina was eventually introduced to, Liam Tracey's boyfriend. Apparently, Liam offered to give Tina a lift home from Tracey's house one night after visiting. He decided to give her a lot more than just a lift. Apparently, they were at it in the back of his van. My sister found out and when she told me I was livid. How could my friend do that to my sister? Word got round that I was going to thump her one and we were soon in the school office being firmly spoken to. My so-called mate steered clear of me.

A meeting was called for in May due to Mrs A 's concern over how much time Mark was spending at Parkside with me. She was sick of the sight of him and I accused her of hating him. I was upset with her and went to see Mum a few times to talk to her. She was OK with me. The meeting went very well. I was in control and had a civilised conversation about visitation limits. Mark and I discussed sharing meals at my new flat when I got it and he agreed to give me some money towards the cost.

I called home again one evening to see Mum. I was having a heated discussion with Mum over something in the kitchen. Right on cue Tracey came down the stairs and said nastily: "Get back to care, where you belong!"

Those razor-sharp words cost her a smack in the mouth. She landed on the floor in front of Mum who told me to get out of the house. Before I left I stated that I was in care for doing a lot less than her. I knew Tracey was now causing a lot of problems at home and I wasn't going to be made a scapegoat any more.

Just a few days before my sixteenth birthday, I moved

in to my flat at Parkside. Just outside the main building were two houses split into four flats. My flat was on the ground floor. I was made up. I had my own living area and bedroom and shared the kitchen. I kept it clean and enjoyed cooking my own meals. I was quite adventurous. I received an allowance for food and laundry and went shopping at Moreton Cross once a week. I was allowed to have a party in my flat for my sixteenth birthday and I was in my element. I felt the bee's knees at my age in my own flat entertaining guests. Rules and regulations still applied of course but I felt as if a weight had been lifted from my shoulders.

My birthday arrived and my loyal school friends came around to my party. Mark wasn't there. He had been ignoring me again and he didn't know I had moved in to my flat. I had a cracking time without him. My favourite film had been *Dirty Dancing* after seeing it with Debbie and we belted the records out in my little living room. We danced and had the time of our lives. All good fun and no problems. Happy memories.

My exams came and went. I struggled with French but flew through home economics and art. I still didn't know what I wanted to do but I had a few ideas. I was good at cooking and thought I could do craft catering at college. I liked the idea of making wedding cakes and decorating them. I had applied for painting and decorating and bricklaying, but they must have thought it was a joke, me being a girl and only one of them replied. I got myself an interview at college for the craft catering course. I was very nervous but very thorough taking my exam results with me and looking smart. I was called in to an office at the college by a stern looking man. He looked up and down at my results. He ummed and ahhd a bit. I had passed all my GCSEs (*even French*) and he proceeded to tell me that I was overqualified with these results and maybe the general catering was a better option for me. *Overqualified??*

In my head I was screaming 'No! I don't want to do that!'

I said nothing. I would only get in to trouble. The general catering included the reception and academic side and was a longer course to boot. I went along with the man's suggestions and was placed on to the general catering course due to start in September.

My move to the flat across from Parkside was going really well. One of my fond memories of it was sitting in my living room Sunday evenings on my own with a bottle of wine and watching *Anne of Green Gables*. I absolutely adored it and still do. I sobbed into my wine glass at the romantic moments and relished every minute of this luscious story. My only problem at my flat now was Mark spending far too much time there and it was getting me in to trouble. I was making him his meals and staff complained he was eating all my food and that I was looking ill. I didn't mind sharing my food. I would feed anyone who comes to my house still to this day. He also stayed over a lot knowing he shouldn't have been there. He was caught one night in my bed. I was bound to get in trouble again for that even though I was now sixteen.

The arguments between us were becoming more violent now and he was hitting me on a regular basis. One particular incident was when he decided he was leaving me again, which happened regularly. He had acquired a mountain bike from somewhere (which turned out to be stolen from his best friend from Southport) and was about to jump on it and ride off. I grabbed at the bike's seat to stop him going and it came off in my hand. He couldn't leave without the seat so I ran with it, straight out of my front door. He ran after me across the grass at the front of the houses which were in front of the home and he grabbed me, throwing me to the ground. I started screaming hysterically as he hit me. He pulled at the seat but I was not letting go of it. Everyone came out to stand and watch. I felt stupid and made a total fool of myself but I couldn't stop screaming. He gripped the seat with two hands, kept one foot on the floor, stood on my chest with the other foot and yanked the seat free. I let him go. I was a shaking mess and covered in mud, cuts and bruises. A member of staff took me in to the staff flat and ran me a bath. I got in to the hot suds and sobbed in to the bath water.

15. College

It was decided to bring me back in to the main building for two weeks, partly as punishment for having Mark stay over and partly for my own health and safety. I was livid about it at first but George asked me to calm down and suggested that I bring it up at my next review. I had adopted a mature attitude for this review which went really well. I agreed I was partly at fault for letting Mark sleep over and I was able to discuss other issues that were bothering me. I said that all I would like was for my Mum to phone me once a week to see how I was. The review went so well that I was allowed to stay in my flat on a last warning.

I had totally forgotten all about the, Tracey, Liam and Tina saga at this stage when it all blew up in my face again. Mum fell out with me again saying I had phoned Liam's father (I can't even remember his name now), making accusations about Liam and Tracey.

Because Liam was eighteen and Tracey was underage, there had been talk of pressing charges against him. Liam's father had forebode him from seeing Tracey altogether to prevent this happening. I wasn't even aware she was still seeing him because after he had slept with Tina I assumed the relationship was finished, but it obviously wasn't. Whoever had phoned Liam's father told him exactly what was going on and it caused a lot of trouble. Guess who was in the firing line? I got the blame for the whole thing. I had never even clapped eyes on Liam's father.

"Why did I do it?" Mum kept asking. She went on about how I had destroyed a lot of relationships, including ours. I insisted I didn't know what she was talking about or even who this man was that she kept saying I'd phoned. She was adamant that it was me. I personally think it was Tina in revenge but I'll never know now. I was heartbroken and Tracey didn't speak to me again for another two years.

I started college in September. I had my new set of Chef's knives and my smart whites and settled in to class for a new start. It was strange at first. I didn't know anybody and there was a lot to take in. But then everyone else was in the same boat as me.

I learned to make a béchamel sauce and memorised all the names of the cuts used in the French language, like a macedoine of carrots and a chiffonade of lettuce. I made steak and kidney pudding and soups and stews. We learned how to run a restaurant, a bakery and to wait on customers, serving their meals and taking their orders. The bakery was heaven on earth. We were in there from eight till eight every Friday making bread and buns and cream cakes. Choux pastry and tarts. I always went home stuffed and feeling very content.

I soon made lots of friends there and found I got on much better with the boys than I did with the girls. I would invite the boys in turns for tea at my flat and they invited me to their homes too. It was lovely to be in a family environment. One boy I met introduced me to INXS, who were to become my favourite group of all time. He invited me to his house and his sister made pasta a la carbonara. I sat at the table with his family to eat my meal and felt at ease with them.

It was only a few days after my last review meeting and Mark was caught in my flat again one morning after he'd stayed by 'Ankle-chain Annie. 'Ankle-chain Annie as we christened her was one of the night staff who seemed to always have the police around to visit when she was on duty, and of course she wore an ankle chain. Mark and I had made up after the big fight we'd had and we were back together so he'd stayed the night.

I'd blown it now with my flat. Stupid me.

I was brought back in to the main building this time. I was given the flat next door to the one Mark used to occupy. Kara now lived in his old flat and we became friends. I was secretly pleased that I had been moved in to this flat because here I was on my own and I hadn't been getting on with Debbie who I had been sharing with. We loved each other to bits but living with her was a different kettle of fish. Mum was refusing to even speak to me, still adamant that it was me that had telephoned Liam's Dad. She said I had ruined friendships.

By October Mark and I had split up again. As usual I chased after him and pleaded for us to get back together but he chose to ignore me. I felt trapped in a way because I had slept with him and believed we were now bound together. Because I'd been pregnant I felt like I had to make it work with him. I went to his flat to talk things over and he would always be out. Normally our splits would last for a few days or even up to a week and then we would get back together again, but not this time. Some members of staff had often said to me over the last year and ten months not to run after him. They said to play hard to get and he would come running after me. I never wanted to take the risk. I was so scared of losing him. After about four weeks I gave up chasing him. I wasn't getting anywhere. He wasn't coming back this time. It was over!

I threw myself in to college life and found I quite enjoyed it. I was invited to parties and started to get part-time work in restaurants nearer to Christmas. I saved my money and I had two bell jars that I put pound coins in. I bought my own coffee percolator and a kettle amongst other kitchen appliances. I had my own bedding and stereo. I was very domesticated and also had a bottom drawer. I saw a few sneaky ways of making some money too. Instead of using my laundry money to go and do my washing at a public laundrette, I would sneak it in to the homes laundry room when no one was looking and throw it in to the machine there. Quite convenient now my flat was in the main building .I only had to go down the stairs.

Another thing was stealing food from the kitchen. Well I say stealing! Marks and Spencer used to donate all the food just going out of date and it would be sent to various charities and homes. When the crates of food came in, they were left stacked up in the kitchen. Debbie and I had a knack of pushing the kitchen's hatch door open, climbing in and grabbing what we could and then dived back out through the hatch. I think we did it more out of fun than anything else. I have never laughed so hysterically as the times when we used to try to climb the stairs to my flat door. Our arms would be laden so full with cheese and ham-sandwiches and posh yogurts, pies and fresh cream cakes. We had to be careful with the bottled milk though as we were laughing so much we would be dropping things. Every time we picked something up, something else would fall off the pile. Hilarious! That just made us laugh even more. The milk would be strategically placed under the stairs and we would come back to it later. Well, it had been donated to us anyway! I saved a bit on the shopping money then to put in my jars.

I was starting to get over Mark and found a new love interest at college. A gorgeous boy who I swore was Elvis's love child. He was tall with dark hair, very quiet and mysterious. It wasn't long before we kissed at a friend's engagement party. I had saved my money and bought a new suit in gold satin and black lace. It was stunning and I felt beautiful... until I stood up and put my high heel through the lace at the bottom of the skirt! I sewed it up and it still looked fabulous. I went to the party and everyone commented on my gorgeous outfit and I slow danced with my new beau. I never quite got together with him, but he certainly took my mind off Mark.

Another boy, John, whom I was very friendly with in the brotherly sense, had invited me to stay over. I had met his family a number of times and they had taken me in with open arms. His Mum had always wanted a girl and I think she thought of me fondly. She invited me to be a part of her family for Christmas.

In November I decided to go and see Dad. I hadn't seen him for ages and I didn't want him to think I had forgotten him, or was not interested in seeing him any more. I jumped on the bus and went into town. It was a freezing cold day and I wrapped up warm. I got to the block of flats and heard a right racket going on. The whole tower block was surrounded by scaffolding and rubble. Workmen with hard hats on were at the scene which resembled a builder's yard. I still didn't twig what was happening and tried to look for a way in to my dads flat. A work man from quite high up the tower block shouted down:

"Are you alright, love?"

I shouted up, "Yeah, I'm just trying to get in to see me Dad."

"Where does he live, love?"

"On the top floor."

"No, no-one lives here now love, the flats are being knocked down."

My Dad had gone. He'd moved away and hadn't even told me he was going. I walked away from the empty flats feeling just as empty as they were. The tears stung my face because it was so cold out. I blamed myself for not contacting him sooner and wished to God I had done so.

16. A Fabulous Christmas

I kept my flat spotless and George was impressed. Mark's absence was doing me the world of good, allowing me to get on with my life. My temperament improved and I was a lot happier. I had several Christmas parties lined up and bought another beautiful new dress to go out in. George had seen Mum, who told him she had now realised that I had not been involved in phoning Liam's father. She wondered why I hadn't tried to tell her the truth. I had tried, she just hadn't been listening!

She wrote me a letter (which she often did) and wanted to clear the air and make plans for the festive season. I was very pleased with the letter I received and excitedly showed it to a member of staff. I called in to see Mum shortly after that with a friend from college as she had clearly waved the white flag. To my disappointment, Mum wanted to discuss the whole Liam and Tracey thing again. I just wanted to forget it. I suggested to her that we just let it lie as it was not worth bringing it up again. Mum insisted. I was very civilised and had acted in a mature manner, but when I refused to talk about it she told me to leave. She later cancelled another of my visits because of this.

I told George what had happened and he said how sorry he was that it had happened in that way. He telephoned Mum to put my point across but she snapped at him accusing him of taking sides. She said Tina had written a letter to her accusing me of the whole horrible thing and it all blew up again. She slammed the phone down on George after telling him not to bother visiting her again. Mrs A was told about these further developments and she was surprised by Mum's reactions too as I had shown her the nice letter I had received only the day before. I was even more confused by her actions.

I busied myself with Christmas and bought my own tree for the flat. I was excited because I had received permission to stay with John's family for two days over the holidays. I had no other plans in place and Mum hadn't invited me home so I jumped at the chance. They made such a fuss of me when I got there and the youngest son had even vacated his bedroom for the night so I could sleep there. I slept in his cabin bed and remember feeling how lucky I was to stay here with this lovely family.

John and I were very close but I didn't think of him in the boyfriend way. He was more like a brother, as were his three brothers. I always gave him a kiss goodbye on his rosy cheek when I went back home from being at his house. I had made him Spaghetti Bolognese at my flat one night and we laughed as the spaghetti slapped us round the face when we sucked it up. Our cheeks were covered in tomato sauce. I think his Mum always hoped we would get together one day and thought of me as a daughter but I was happy to just be friends with John.

Christmas day was fabulous. There was a real family atmosphere. I woke up to presents at the bottom of my bed, *lots* of them. I hadn't expected all that. I spent the day with them and had Christmas dinner. They treated me as their own and I have never forgotten them for it.

On New Year's Eve I had a private work function at Hulme hall. I was waiting on (waitress service) with a few friends from college. It was all good fun. Even funnier when one of the boys slipped on spilt gravy and a whole flat of chicken was tossed straight over his head as he landed on his bottom. Poor Nat!! He sat on the floor amongst the mess while five hundred party goers applauded him.

After Christmas, Mum was annoyed and disappointed that I hadn't contacted her or sent her a Christmas card. She failed to see that her not sending me a card or contacting me was in any way a problem.

January 1989 brought me the flu and a knock at my door. To my surprise it was Mark with his tail between his legs. I hadn't seen him now for at least six weeks and I had moved on. I had learned to live without him in this time and that there was a world beyond him. The strange thing was, now that I didn't want him anymore, he wanted me. All this time, people had told me not to chase him and he would come back. All the times they said play hard to get and I could never bring myself to do it. They had been right. Mark begged me to take him back and I felt so guilty. I didn't want to hurt him despite the way he had treated me so I did get back with him. For the next week he tried really hard to make it up to me but whenever he touched me I was sick to the stomach. I kept on seeing him until I'd worked out how I really felt and to see if these feelings would go away. He called to see me one night and he put his arms round my waist from behind like a kind of bear hug. I flinched. That was it, I couldn't stand him touching me anymore. We had gone well past our sell-by date. Even so I still didn't want to hurt him and I tried to be sensitive.

I told him, "It's no good. I just don't feel the same about you any more."

This time it really was the end and for once, it was me that ended it.

The next three months went really well. I went to college daily and progressed to the stage where I felt it was time for me to move on. I was ready for a real flat of my own. The offer of a hostel came my way with help from Parkside and it seemed like the natural progression. I saved and saved and altogether put two hundred pound coins in my bell jars. I opened a bank account and I put some of the money in for a rainy day. I asked George if he had heard anything from Mum. He said he hadn't, as his visits had now ceased altogether. Mum blamed him for our lack of communication and said he had tried to split the family up so she no longer wished him to visit. There was also no news of my Dad's whereabouts which bothered me a lot. I was angry. Why did he just cut me off like that?

I commented at the news, *'Both my parents can eff-off now, they don't want to know me anyway, I was an accident anyway and shouldn't have happened.'*

My neighbour Kara had moved out and my new neighbour Sally had moved in. Sally was a very quiet girl but you didn't mess with her. She was tall and beautiful with short blonde curls. We got on like a house on fire and sometimes we went out for a drink together. I sat in

A Fabulous Christmas

her flat now and again and we listened to *The Lost Boys* sound track from the film. We were good friends then and remain so today.

I moved to, Home Base on 14th March 1989. I was really sad to leave Parkside. It was my home, but on the other hand I knew I had to move on at some point. I packed up all my belongings, shoving a lot of things in my washing basket. It was all very last-minute preparation and Mary my key worker wasn't even there to say goodbye. I was rushed but excited too. I clutched my washing basket and took my final journey down the stairs that we hid the milk under, down the corridor, past the staff office and past the laundry room where I'd lost so many socks and I later used to sneak my washing in.

Mrs A still had to get the last word in, asking me, "Is that **our** washing basket you're taking?"

Not 'Goodbye' or 'Good luck', just 'Have you pinched our washing basket?'

I looked at her in disgust and replied, "No, it's mine, I bought it with my own money!" I waltzed off and jumped into the waiting car. Goodbye to you!

The hostel I moved in to, Home Base, as it was called was three houses in central Birkenhead. The middle house had an office downstairs where staff were on duty twenty four hours a day. The houses were three bed roomed so three girls in each house had their own bedroom and shared the kitchen and bathroom. College was only two minutes down the road so that was very handy for me. The staff at Home Base were brilliant. I settled in straight away and they were very pleased indeed with me.

In June I was taking my catering exams. I was starting to find it very difficult at college and wondered if I really wanted a career in the kitchen. I was stuck in a hot sweaty kitchen in the beautiful summer weather. I had originally wanted to do the craft side of catering but this course was more the academic side, which had never appealed to me. I hated the hotel reception part of the course and the bakery on a Friday was heaven but a killer too, starting at eight in the morning ending at eight in the evening. The cream cakes and bread were good, though!

I managed to miss one of my exams as I had been told by one of the other students it was in the afternoon. When I got there it had already taken place in the morning. Another exam I failed – not good!

I had always been a very clean person but now I was sharing with two other girls at Home Base and it seemed an impossible task. Whenever I went to the kitchen to make something to eat, the pots, pans and dishes would be stacked up in the sink and the plates and dirty dishes would be everywhere. Bins were never emptied, the bath was left in a disgusting mess with a ring round it and the same happened with the twin tub. I could never do my washing until I'd emptied somebody else's filthy, frothy brown water out of it first.

One day I came in and I could see a mist in the living room. I thought nothing of it and went to my bedroom with my sister. We were up there for a good twenty minutes playing music and chatting. When I came back out of the bedroom the whole house was full of thick smoke and the smell of burning. I ran down to the kitchen and found a pan of what had been savoury rice blackened and now welded to the bottom of a melting pan. My house mate had put it on the stove and left the building before I had even arrived. I had been upstairs all that time and there was still no sign of her. She could have burnt the whole house down.

Another occasion the same girl went out and got rotten drunk on vodka and coke. She came in and threw up on the living room carpet. I swear it was still there two weeks later. She was disgusting. Needless to say, she was soon moved on and I got a new housemate.

My new house mate was Debbie, my best friend who had come to join me from Parkside. She had decided to follow me to Home Base too. It was decided as I was so well behaved and managed well that Debbie and I would be moved to a flat ten minutes down the road. It was still part of the Home Base project but there were no staff on site. It was just a normal flat in a normal block. If we needed the staff for anything they were ten minutes away. It was brilliant. Debbie and I were so excited.

We moved in during the summer holidays, when I had just turned seventeen. I bought my own settee, a new hi-fi system and a video recorder with the money I had saved in my jars. I had all my kitchen things packed away ready and really made the new flat my own. Pete, my new boyfriend, came along and helped me to move in. The first week we were there we did get in to trouble for blasting the stereo too much but we soon calmed down after our initial excitement.

I had met Pete at Home Base a few weeks before. He was one of a group of boys visiting a friend there. He lived half an hour up the road from Home Base in another hostel that was run by the same Housing Association. It was the last day of term when we met and I had been over the road in the local pub for a drink. I had been with Elvis's love child that afternoon but it didn't look like we were ever going to get together so I gave up with him. I had come back home with him but he didn't stay long.

I was laying on the couch in my living room watching TV when Pete walked in. I noticed him straight away because he was not so much handsome, but attractive. He was clean looking and had on a pair of jeans and a black and yellow sweater. His hair was a mass of thick dark brown curls and the ends were tinged with grown out peroxide blonde. He had a goatee beard and a smiley face. Pete was sixteen, younger than me and he was in a hostel because he had problems at home too. We had this in common and started seeing each other almost immediately.

Pete was always round at my flat and if we weren't there we were at his flat. He walked me home in the evenings and we cooked meals for each other. He had a part time job in the fair in New Brighton where I would frequent with him throughout the summer. It wasn't long before Pete took me home to meet his family. He was one of six children, two girls and four boys. Things were still no different with my family so I lovingly latched on to his, especially his Dad. They accepted me in to their fold happily. At last I had a new family.

17. A New Family

Pete and I had such a laugh with Debbie and her boyfriend, who was also called Pete. We would call them *my Pete* and *your Pete*. Debbie and I had been like sisters all these years. We had bunked school together, gone on long bus rides and hidden in each others' wardrobes at night so that the staff at Parkside couldn't find us. I found it hard to conceal my giggles from inside the wardrobe when they would ask "Have you seen Gina?" We sometimes jumped in to the bath together too.

The boys had brought some big bottles of lager home to the flat one night which we whipped out of the fridge when they weren't looking and took them in to the bathroom with us. We lay there in the suds and roared with laughter and chatted for ages. By the time we got out of the bath it was black with fag ash and we were both rotten drunk. Things were great for a few weeks but then we started to fall out over the cleaning and food and things.

I had been at my Pete's flat one day when a staff member came up and told us that Debbie had been rushed to hospital after taking an overdose. We rushed straight out and made a beeline for the bus stop to go to the hospital. I know things were strained between us but she was my best friend. I was worried sick. I couldn't help thinking Debbie didn't seem that down to me. She's not the type to OD. We jumped the bus anyway which by chance took us past my flat and when I looked out of the bus window I saw Debbie's Pete's car parked outside. Surely he would have taken her to the hospital so why was his car there? Something wasn't quite right. Someone was playing games with us. We jumped off the bus and ran back to my flat to find a clueless Debbie and Pete sitting there. They didn't have any idea what I was talking about when I asked if she was OK. We left the flat none the wiser.

When we got back to Pete's flat we were immediately told that our video player had been stolen. On checking the flat it most certainly had. Then we put two and two together. We had been sent on a wild goose chase so that our video recorder could be stolen. We had been set up.

The summer holidays ended and it was time to go back to catering college. Debbie and I had fallen out and she decided to move out with her Pete. We'd had some great laughs together but we just couldn't live together. Not long after moving out she discovered she was pregnant. Pete and I had the flat to our selves now and enjoyed the time alone. I would often give him my cash card to nip to the bank and take a fiver out and go to the chippy for our tea. The chip shop over the road from us was fantastic. We were always given a huge orange or apple with our meal.

One night, we were having a night in and there was a loud banging at the front door. I went to answer it and Pete's brother was standing there in a rage. He started shouting about his wallet. I was totally flummoxed. What the hell was he on about? Pete came to the door then and there was an altercation about some money that had gone missing from his brother's wallet. He eventually left after putting his fist straight through the glass window in my front door. I didn't have a clue what it was all about.

Shortly after that I came back from town shopping one day to find two girls knocking on my door. I was alarmed at first because I didn't know who they were and I was suspicious of them. I became most annoyed when one of the girls announced she would be moving in with me. I didn't know anything about it. I didn't think it was fair to move someone in with me that I didn't know. It was just sprung on me and I had no say in the matter. The girl seemed alright though so that was a relief. The staff later explained that I wouldn't be able to stay at my flat on my own anyway now that Debbie had moved out as it was designed to be shared accommodation.

The girl moved in and it didn't take long for it to become an absolute nightmare. My flat turned in to the red light district. I would come home from college and there were boys there that I didn't know lounging on my sofa. The carpet had one long huge beer stain from the alcohol that had been spilt at the foot of the settee. There were parties till all hours and boys staying over. Her friend then ran away from home and moved in with her. My food was repeatedly taken out of the cupboards and I ended up locking all my belongings away in my bedroom. I came in one day to find the gas fire on full blast and a maiden full of clothes virtually on top of it. I wouldn't have minded so much but no one was at home! Very dangerous!

I complained about them.

Both girls made my life a misery from then on. I was

relieved when I came back from college a few days later to find them on the path outside moving out with all their stuff. They shouted a few obscenities at me and then they left when their taxi came. I ignored them and went upstairs to my flat. To my horror when I got up there they had kicked my bedroom door open and stolen half of my belongings including my kettle and my bedding. I found a nasty letter that they had composed to me lying on my bed. It said that I wasn't to tell anyone what they had done or *'We will kill you like you killed your baby,'* and *'We're not scared of your beastie boyfriend.'*

To say I was devastated was an understatement. Debbie must have told them about my termination in her anger at me. I didn't care about the kettle or the bedding; it was their words that had cut me deeply. How can people say such cruel things to one another?

I wasn't going to let them get away with it though so I did report them to the staff. Pete had also read the letter and he comforted me. Luckily we had shared all our secrets and he knew all about what I had been through at Parkside. He didn't judge me.

That vicious girl came back a few days later for her Giro as it would have been sent to our address. It wasn't there. She swore blind I had taken it and shouted at me to "Give me my money back!"

I had not seen any letters addressed to her at all. I did receive a letter shortly after that though………..my bank statement. I looked it over casually but something didn't quite look right. I knew I should have had more money than that. I checked the transactions that had been made and I didn't believe my eyes at first. I didn't want to believe it. I double checked and I couldn't possibly be wrong. For every single occasion that I had given Pete my cash card for our chippy teas he had taken more money out than I had asked him to. Instead of five pounds each time he had taken either ten or fifteen and had kept the money for himself. He'd been doing it for a while and it amounted to a fair bit. *How could he?*, I trusted him.

I had it out with him and he couldn't deny it so I threw him out of the flat. He stood out side my living room window and pleaded with me to take him back. I went to sit with my neighbour in the downstairs flat while he carried on shouting up at the window.

"I love you - you don't know how much!"

I felt betrayed but I did take him back eventually because I loved him and his family. They were all I had. I would learn later on in our relationship by his own admission that it was he who had been responsible for the theft of his brother's missing money and my ex-flatmate's Giro too.

At Christmas 1989 I worked hard at college and I enjoyed the restaurant part of my course. I liked waiting on and serving the Christmas dinners up in the college's restaurant. It was such a good atmosphere. I had a few private party functions waiting on too so I was able to earn some extra money outside of college. I put up my tree in the flat and made it as festive as possible.

I stayed at Pete's family's house this year on Christmas Eve and we got engaged on Christmas Day. He romantically hid my engagement ring of blue topaz and diamonds in the Christmas tree but I couldn't find it. I had to be given it in the end. His family were very pleased at our engagement and thought I wasn't a bad lot. We had an engagement party on Boxing Day to celebrate. My Mum refused to come. She said because I was only seventeen and the party was in a pub function room that she could not permit herself to be part of my special day. It would be illegal. She didn't want to get in to trouble with the police because I was under age in a pub. I tried to tell her it was a private family function suite and even so I wasn't drinking anyway, but she wouldn't listen and stuck to her decision not to come.

After Christmas, because I was on my own again in the flat I had to move back to Home Base. A new girl moved in to share the house with me and we became good friends. We went clubbing together and shared our cooking making up concoctions like sardine and corn beef stew. I met her aunty and uncle and we babysat for their children. She used to do my hair with a special lotion that she used to get for her afro hair and we shared our clothes and were just daft together. It was around this time I went through a phase of smoking things I shouldn't have been smoking. We partied hard, going out at night and sleeping in the day. We walked home from the clubs at night and were oblivious of ever being in danger.

One night a man offered to walk us home from a night club we'd been at. We declined saying we were fine thank you. He was very persistent and wouldn't take no for an answer. He followed us through town and we hoped he would just disappear if we ignored him. However as we walked past an alley he grabbed my friend and dragged her down the alleyway.

She screamed, "Gina, help me!"

At first I didn't realise what was going on but when I saw she was struggling with him half way down the alley I had to do something. It all happened really quickly. I desperately looked around for anyone to shout to for help. Normally the police would be in their droves in this part of town, but not that night, when they were needed. I ran down the alley and started swinging my handbag at him furiously. The handle was so long it seemed to take ages to swing round and make contact with him.

"Get off, get off her!" I screamed at him in desperation.

He grabbed at my bag as it came flying towards him and we struggled with it. He let go of my friend and everything flew up in the air out of my bag as we both tugged at it. I let go of the bag and took one of my stiletto heels off. I whacked him as hard as I could right across the side of his head. The blood came oozing out and ran down his bare chest where his shirt was open in a long trickle. I looked at where my heel had pierced him in the head and there was a hole. He was stunned enough for me to gather my bag and lipstick and house keys. I took my friends hand and we ran all the way home.

A few weeks later she wasn't so lucky. We had gone to our usual night club and while I was inside she stayed outside talking to a boy we knew. I was wondering where she had got to and came outside to look for her. I was told by the doormen that she had been raped in the car park. She was never the same after that and flipped a few days later, smashing her room up and cutting her self quite badly. It took six policemen to restrain her and take her away. I just looked on in dismay.

College was a real drag and I hated it now. I just didn't want to be there anymore. I started going in to classes late, stoned, and not paying any attention. I decided to leave the course and took up a new care in the community course. I loved it.

I went to college in Wallasey once a week and I had a placement in the day in a nursing home. I met some really nice girls there. The first nursing home I was placed at was awful though. Basically I was used as a dogsbody because I was a trainee. Every single day for weeks was subject to cleaning the same commodes, same sinks and same toilets; upstairs in the morning and downstairs in the afternoon. The monotony was enough to drive anyone round the bend. I sat with the domestics on our morning break who were all lovely to me. They shared their all-butter shortbread with me and poured me a well earned cup of tea. I didn't learn a thing about being a carer.

I had gone to the kitchen one day to ask if I could help serve the morning tea to the ladies. My offer of help was welcomed. I set about organising the cups and saucers and at last felt like I was doing something positive. I picked up the heavy industrial-sized teapot full of scalding hot tea and was about to pour. At that moment the matron walked in holding a pair of black lace up-shoes in the air and spoke to me in a very rude tone.

She said, "Look at these shoes! They're full of dog muck! Eileen can't go out in them like that. Clean them up now please!"

A New Family

I was shocked at the way she spoken to me and unsure whether I should finish what I was doing first or put the teapot down and do it immediately.

My answer was an angry, *"NOW"* from her.

I was dumbfounded. I had kept my nose clean, and the commodes for that matter for weeks now and I felt that I was just there to shovel shite! I put the pot down and waltzed past the matron my eyes filling up with frustrated tears.

At the front door I shouted, *"I'm not your effing skivvy"* and walked out the front door.

I didn't look back when I left. I'd had enough!

I explained to the staff at Home Base what I had done, that I had lost my temper and I'd sworn. I was gutted that it had come to that and I didn't know what to do but I knew I wasn't going back there. I had been treated unfairly. Thankfully I was placed in another nursing home and this one was great. I cleaned bottoms and dressed the ladies. I made beds and served meals. I mucked in the same as everyone else, worked extremely hard and I learned to be a carer.

18. A New Flat

My new college course went really well and before I knew it the summer was fast approaching again. I knew that there was a holiday being organised but I wasn't sure when it was. I think I had been off sick when the letters were handed out in class. I arrived at college bright and early in May one morning and everyone was sat outside with their luggage waiting for the coach ready to go. I hadn't realised it was today and I was too late to go now. My face fell with disappointment at the sight of my friends sitting chatting excitedly. One of the tutors asked me where my things were and I explained I hadn't known the holiday was today. She offered to run me back to Home Base in her car to get permission from the staff for me to go, and so I could pack my things. I felt so excited. I was like a wild woman running about and hurriedly packing my bags when the staff said that I could go. I just made it back to college before the coach left. Yippee!

Llanberis in Wales was fantastic. I shared a chalet with my girl friends from college. I abseiled from a huge cliff, rock climbed, canoed and I climbed to the top of Snowdon. I didn't want to do the abseil at first as I was a bit scared, but then I looked over at the cliff and the others doing it. The urge to just do it nagged at me. I thought that if I didn't do it then, I might regret it later. My attitude seemed to give a few of the other girls who

A New Flat

had backed out the courage to do it too and we all went for it together. I stood at the edge of the cliff and waited my turn and when it came I was harnessed up, I leaned back over the cliff with the instructor's guidance, gripped my rope and went for it. I zipped to the bottom almost letting go of my rope as it burned through my hands. It was exhilarating and I wanted to do it again.

Now the canoeing was a different story. I was petrified. I suppose I more sat very still in the canoe than actually canoed in it. Capsizing was not an option!

We were split in to teams after that experience and were shown how to make a raft with barrels and ropes. We were shown different knots with the ropes and we set about our task. Our raft was great until we pushed it out on the lake and tried to get on to it. It was a hilarious sight with all of us sliding off it one by one and the barrels floating off into the distance. We learned to be part of a team that afternoon and had a scream doing it.

The day we climbed up Mount Snowdon it was a scorcher. I hadn't taken any sun cream with me as I had rushed with my packing and not thought about it. It seemed that no one else had thought about it either as they hadn't banked on the glorious weather. It took us four hours to get to the top of the mountain and about two hours to come back down. It was hard work climbing the steep rocks. We ate our picnic half way up and admired the magnificent views on the way back down. Vast mountain lakes with crystal still waters lay untouched in the depth of the mountains. The burning sun dipped in to its tranquil beauty leaving silver traces on the rippled surface. It was a stunning sight that I have never forgotten.

We were all burnt like crispy bacon two hours later when we descended the mountain. One of the girls had sun stroke and most of us had puffed up eyes. We lay in our bunk beds that night sore and aching whilst writing our postcards. Despite this I had a superb time on this activity holiday and made some good friends.

I turned eighteen in June and Home Base planned a surprise party for me and another boy who was eighteen on the same day. We had a birthday cake each made especially for us. Mine was pale pink and his was pale blue and a spread had been laid on in the middle house. All the residents at Home base were there and a good time was had by all, with music playing and dancing. I went over to the pub when my party had finished. The local pub was only over the road from Home Base and all my friends from school and John from college came to wish me a happy birthday, and to buy me a birthday drink! I was so pleased that I had so many nice friends. I had one over the eight whilst I was in the pub. When I got back home I drunkenly took my lovely pink cake upstairs to my room to show Pete. I dropped it coming back down the stairs to put it away. I managed to catch it before it landed and the icing rippled in the middle as the cake concertinaed. It still tasted delicious though!

Mum had got in touch with me just before my eighteenth birthday too and we were able to put our differences aside for a few weeks. She offered to take me out for the day to a craft centre and to have our lunch there. Tracey came along too and although she still held

A New Flat

me responsible for the Liam saga we were starting to get on a bit. She had even made me a birthday cake and decorated it with pink icing and little plastic silver bows. I thought it was a very sweet gesture. I took photos of it along with my presents. I lent her my jacket to wear as we walked round the craft shops and we had a really nice day out. It was nice us all being together as a family.

A few days after that, we went to see Paul McCartney in concert. Mum and Tracey were fans and had bought tickets for his show. He was doing a homecoming tour in Liverpool and this was to be my eighteenth birthday present. We went over really early to queue up on a hot day in June. We waited all day next to the barriers in the blazing heat. Our neighbour who had come along with us was all togged up in her flower power flairs and shades. She was really funny and the sight of her took some of the monotony away. The gates were opened hours later and we frantically ran in and got right to the front, grabbing goody bags that were being handed out on the way. I remember the film camera on the stage in the distance scanning around the crowds. I watched it for a while and it seemed to be watching me. I blew it a kiss and the camera made a round swooning motion as it acknowledged my gesture. I was ecstatic. All these people here and it had noticed me!

Soon the concert began with a low deep droning sound coming up through the floor. I felt exhilarated and had never been to anything like it. The concert was absolutely fantastic and well worth the wait. We all had a moment there that day as a family.

In August my temper got the better of me again. I

had an argument with a staff member at Home Base and it proved to be one too many. After stupidly banging the office window with my mug in annoyance, I was given my notice. The window didn't smash or anything and I'd had no intention of breaking it, but they didn't see it like that. I was eighteen now anyway and once again it was time for me to move on. I had nowhere to go though so Mum felt she had no option but to take me home for the time being until I had found a flat. She was livid and didn't want me to come back home. I didn't understand. We may not have got on in the past but we had been fine over my birthday and we'd had a great time. What was the problem?

I packed my belongings and went to stay at Mum's. I felt really awkward as I knew how the story would go being back at home. I could feel the tension in the air and I knew I wasn't wanted there. I had my own fridge freezer that I'd bought for twenty pounds from someone and she was furious that it would have to sit in the back garden till I got my flat. She walked around with a face like a wet weekend. I did my best to cheer her up and to let her know that I wasn't there to cause trouble. My efforts were in vain though and I felt rejected all over again.

I jumped on the bus in the mornings to my placement in Birkenhead and I kept well out of Mum's way. I wasn't working in the nursing home any more as my placement there had ended. I had been moved to a day care hospital for the elderly, which was just up the road from Home Base. I used to make the jam sandwiches up here in the morning for the ladies. Up until I moved back to Mum's house I'd been stuffing my self with the jam butties as I was starving every morning. I'd had to keep my food

A New Flat

locked in my room at Home Base. You couldn't leave anything lying around or in the kitchen cupboards as it got pinched and there was only so much you could hide in a bedroom in the summer heat. I lived on Mini-Cheddars or dry crackers. Even if you could leave your food in the kitchen you couldn't cook anything because it was always like a bombsite. I remember getting caught with a mouthful of sandwich one day by the matron. She knew I had my mouth full and she asked me a question about something and I had to give her a muffled answer. At least at Mum's I didn't have to hide my food anymore!

Pete and I had split up after a row just before my birthday so he had no idea I was staying at my mums. As far as I was concerned we were over. I wouldn't see him again and that was fine by me. I wasn't ever going to chase a man again after what had happened with Mark

I was at Mum's for two weeks before I was offered a flat on the Ford Estate, now called the Beechwood Estate. I wasn't happy about it to begin with because the place held a lot of bad memories. Mum said she would throw me out if I didn't take it so I had no option. I hadn't seen George now since last October and was introduced to my new social worker, a lady called June. I don't think she thought very much of me and she criticised me quite a lot. She was to assist me with my move to my new home. She was nice enough but she was a fuss-pot and it really got on my nerves.

The flat was situated within a small block of flats and had one bedroom. It was a disgrace when I went to view it and needed a lot of work doing to it. Tracey came and helped me to clean it up but my heart just wasn't in it. I moved in on 9th August 1990.I was lucky enough to be entitled to both a decorating grant and a leaving care grant so I went shopping for paint and wall paper, curtains and a bed. I was given a cooker and had my fridge moved from Mum's back garden, much to her delight. I decorated the flat myself and found I quite enjoyed it. I was also allocated a home-maker, to help me with the decorating but I turned out to be a dab hand anyway. I got a paste table and set about making my wall paper paste, following the instructions very carefully. I matched my paper up and brushed the squidgy glue on, thoroughly enjoying it. I put far too much paste on at first and it soaked through the paper leaving wet patches but I quickly got the hang of it. The home-maker was a great help and I liked him a lot. I had bought an old solid wood dressing table and a matching tallboy from an auction and he stripped them down and polished them with a special wax. He was truly an expert and spent hours sanding and polishing. Underneath their coat of mahogany varnish they turned out to be beautiful red cedar wood and they came up absolutely beautifully. I sadly sold them on a few weeks later in favour of a modern white set of dressing table and chest of drawers. One of those stupid things you do when you're young then later regret. My poor home-maker was gutted after all his hard work.

I had only been at my flat for two weeks and a TV license man knocked at the door. He was enquiring about the previous occupant who obviously hadn't had a license. I explained to him I had just moved in and had only had my TV for two days. I hadn't had a chance to get a license yet. I didn't even have a settee or carpets down. I was

A New Flat

greeted the following week with a fine on my doorstep. So much for understanding!

A few days after that I was very surprised when Pete knocked on my door. I wasn't expecting to see him ever again. He had been looking for me and had got my address from Mum. I hadn't wanted to get back with him but I invited him in to talk, and things went from there. I was lonely in the flat and it was nice to have him around. He made me laugh with his, Pob impressions. (Pob was a children's cartoon character). He moved in shortly after and we talked about having a baby. I wasn't sure if I could still get pregnant after the termination and I desperately wanted the family that I felt I had never had. I was very young and naïve. He moved in and I invited Pete's Mum to the flat for tea one evening and his little brother came too.

I made one of my Mum's favourite recipes, fish pie. You put a layer of tuna on the bottom of a casserole dish, a layer of sliced hard-boiled eggs on top of that. Next a layer of creamed mushrooms and then creamy mashed potatoes on the top of that. Mmm!

My home-maker was really easy to talk to and I told him of my plans for a baby. He bothered to talk to me and get to know me. He really understood. He offered me some good advice about waiting till I was ready. I told him I had a bottom drawer with a few baby things in it that I had put away for when the time came.

I said to him, "I will never do to my child what my Mum has done to me,"

He replied, "Well, what will you do instead, though?"

A good point I thought!

He mentioned to another home-maker that I would benefit from some counselling and noted that I had unmet needs with regards to my Mum.

He was told to *'Leave it alone, it's up to Gina if she feels she needs that level of aid.'*

I *did* need that level of aid!

What a shame I wasn't offered it. I didn't know it was available to me, so how could I ask for it?

Despite advice from my home-maker for the next few months I tried to get pregnant but nothing happened. I was sure I wouldn't be able to have children now as a punishment from God for what I had done. Each month I would cry when I realised I definitely wasn't.

19. A Baby Girl

I put getting pregnant to the back of mind for the time being and that's exactly when it happened. In November I was a few days late and I hoped that I was. I put a test in at the doctors and waited for two days for the results. Pete and I were in Birkenhead when I phoned the surgery from a phone kiosk in the outside market. The secretary announced over the phone that my test was positive. I cried with relief and happiness at the news. My due date was 23rd June 1991 and I just knew I was going to have a girl.

I remained at college to finish my course. As the first few weeks went by I got sicker and sicker.

Morning sickness? It was all flipin day sickness! I would grab a carton of strawberry juice on the way to college and sit in class feeling tired and ill. The only things I could eat were salt and vinegar Chip sticks by the bag full and mashed or baked potatoes with steak and kidney pudding. After college I would walk around the shops and pick up baby items to put in my bottom drawer. I was given a lovely white Broderie Anglaise baby nest to put away too.

We shared our baby news with Pete's Mum and she was thrilled. She was excited at the prospect of a girl too as she already had a grandson from Pete's sister but no granddaughters yet. Tracey visited the flat and I told her the news.

I announced to her, "You're going to be an aunty!"

She seemed pretty pleased but Mum's reaction when Tracey told her was "Oh, the silly girl!"

Mum just assumed the worst of me that it mustn't have been meant to happen. I hoped that my having a baby would bring us closer together now. She was going to be a grandmother for the first time and I wanted us to be a family. I went to see Debbie who'd had her baby in July. She was living with her Pete's Mum and doing really well. She was made up for us both and gave us some of her baby things that she'd finished with. She gave us a playpen that was hardly used and we bought her mint green combo pram from her as she had bought a new one.

I was discharged from care in December. No more social workers or home-makers. Just me in the big wide world, the way I wanted it. With Christmas on its way again I decided on a real Christmas tree this year. The smell of fresh pine would fill the air and give a real festive feel. I didn't feel very festive when we carried it home over a bridge with gale force winds blowing me sideways, though! I had to stop halfway over the bridge. I sat down on the pavement pulled my knees up and cried with exhaustion. Stupid tree. I just wanted to leave it there. Half the needles had blown out in the wind now anyway. Whatever possessed me to carry a tree home in the first place?

Over Christmas I developed a nasty rash all over my body. My arms, legs, elbows and bottom were thick with a horrible raised itching redness. I swore it was the cursed Christmas tree's fault and I was allergic to it. I went to the doctor and was referred to a skin specialist but told there was a wait. By the time I had an appointment I'd have had the baby. It turned out to be some kind of pregnancy eczema and I had to smother myself in a special cream. It didn't do any good!

I became really close with Pete's family at this time and his Mum was very good to me. She went with me to a car boot sale one Sunday morning. I picked up a gorgeous white baby girl's dress on one stall and I had to have it.

Irene said to me: "You don't want to buy anything just yet, not till you know what you're having!"

I looked back at her, smiled and said, "I'm having a girl, I know I am!"

I bought the dress and put it in my bottom drawer which was now expanding rapidly. Irene also taught me how to crochet and make blankets. She would buy me bags of wool to keep me occupied. I picked up wool from charity shops too. I made several blankets sitting in the back yard in the spring sunshine along with Irene, and I finished them off with bows and rosebuds. They were beautiful and I enjoyed making them. Pete's sister lent us her Moses basket and we picked up a cheap cot and painted it. We were all ready for our baby.

Fifteen weeks before my baby was due my college course finished. I had been placed on a college course with other pregnant girls. We had made our own jewellery and did other beneficial activities but that had ended after a few weeks too. I had passed all my exams and received my certificates but what was I going to do now? I was six months pregnant so no-one was going to employ me now and I couldn't claim income support until I had only eleven weeks of pregnancy left. I had to go on sickness benefit for four weeks.

I carried my baby through the June heat and I had my nineteenth birthday. I sat outside my kitchen window in the blazing sun with a magazine and put my feet up on my bright orange pouf to rest. I was eager for my little girl to be born. I imagined her to look like me with blonde hair and blue eyes and how I would have the family I had always craved. I was blooming and in good spirits. I passed my due date and that's when I started to get backache and feel really tired. Irene insisted that I went to stay at her house as Pete was working and I was on my own in the daytime. I packed a few things and stayed at her house and slept in Pete's younger sister's high cabin bed. I climbed in and out of it on a chair. His Dad joked the night before telling me to eat a plum and that would get my labour going. I went to bed exhausted and was up and down all night to the loo. The next morning I was in pain but I didn't want to disturb or wake anyone up. I was sleeping between my contractions. At six thirty I had a show and I knew then that she was coming. I woke Irene up quietly and very soon the whole house was bustling with excitement. Irene timed my contractions with a bemused face.

She felt across my hardening tummy and muttered, "that cant be right."

On realisation that my contractions were only every five minutes apart so I was rushed off to hospital in the

A Baby Girl

family car. I had been in labour all night and not realised it! On the way there Pete's panic stricken Dad nearly knocked the postman over!

When I arrived at the hospital I was taken on to the labour ward. They took my blood pressure and did some routine checks to confirm I was in labour. The pain soon started kicking in. Gas and air is one of man's greatest inventions. I laughed all the way through my labour joking about the price of Jersey Royal potatoes. The midwife said if she had known how well the birth was going to go they would have videoed me for the ante-natal class.

My baby daughter, Coral, was born at 1:36 in the afternoon of 28th June 1991. I was handed my beautiful baby girl all wrapped up in a hospital blanket and already sucking her thumb. I stared down at her little face and tried to absorb the moment but I was lost with the affect of the pethidine. She didn't look anything like me at all. She looked like her Dad with a dark brown mop of hair and a rosy complexion. I wasn't sure how I was supposed to feel and a wave of panic washed over me. Up until this point I had been eager to have my baby and was excited to be starting my own family. I felt that it was expected of me to smile and be happy now but inside I didn't feel like that at all. I held on to my baby and masked my fears. I was in the hospital for a few days with my new baby girl and I struggled, not knowing how to look after her and too scared to ask anyone for help. I was scared to leave her and scared to go to sleep in case something happened to her. Eventually, I at one point went to the toilet and fainted from exhaustion. I should have pulled the emergency cord but felt I would be causing trouble so I dragged myself on my knees to the door.

When I got home I didn't have a clue what I was doing there either. I was prepared for her materially but not mentally. I didn't even know how to prepare her feeds. I had wanted to feed her myself but no one seemed to encourage me to do it so I didn't even try. I had got up in the early hours one night as Coral was hungry and needed a feed. I hadn't realised you could prepare milk earlier and store it in the fridge. Dazed I started from scratch all the while Coral was screaming for her feed. I poured boiling water in to the bottle, scooped in the milk, screwed on the lid and shook it. *Big mistake!!* The bottle exploded with the pressure. Scalding hot milk showered my face and chest and I dropped the bottle on the floor in shock. I was burnt and useless. I collapsed to the floor in a crying mess. What made things worse was that Pete never got up in the night for her to give me a break and he didn't take any time off work to help me either. I couldn't believe he'd got himself a new job the very day that the baby was born and was going straight into work when I needed him. It caused friction between us and resulted in us being at loggerheads with each other. His Mum argued his point saying we needed the money. The funny thing was, I never saw any of it.

I was shattered. Every time I put my head down to rest the midwife or some one else knocked on the front door. I didn't sleep for days. When I had the opportunity to sleep I couldn't because I was petrified something would happen to the baby. I was extremely depressed and then felt guilty for feeling depressed. I couldn't cope. This should have been the happiest time of my life. What the hell was wrong with me? I stopped eating and I cried constantly. I was too scared to tell anyone how I felt in

A Baby Girl

case my baby was taken away from me. Tracey called to see me and Coral one day and as she walked in I leaned against the wall of my flat and slid down to the floor in a heap. I was a complete wreck. Tracey offered to have Coral for an hour or two whilst I had a lay down but I still couldn't sleep for worrying.

When Coral was six weeks old I went to the doctor to get help. In a state I had put her down on the changing mat quite roughly and I was scared of accidentally hurting her. The doctor diagnosed severe post natal depression and she prescribed anti depressants for me. I didn't want to take them at first as I didn't want to end up like my Mum, relying on tablets, but I needed the help.

I stayed with Irene for a week or so until I felt slightly better but she ended up taking over, making me feel even more useless. She meant well but I didn't appreciate her putting colic drops in Coral's bottle of water. I emptied it down the sink when she wasn't looking. I was so grateful for her help that I felt I couldn't tell her that there were certain little things I would have liked to have done differently. I started to feel better when I went back home and I made an effort, taking Coral out for walks in her pram and trying to enjoy her. I always dressed her immaculately with frilly dresses, matching knickers and little mop hats. She was even mistaken for a doll one day when we went to have her photos taken in Birkenhead.

Pete and I got married in September, when Coral was just eight weeks old. I had decided when she was born to make things official and we had booked the wedding then. Pete tended to just go along with things and was easily persuaded. We were very young and had our problems but we were a family now and I believed it to be the right thing to do. I loved him and I wanted our relationship to work, despite our frequent rows. I wanted to make my Mum proud of me too. I admit it was all a bit of a rush. Maybe I was looking for ways to pull myself out of my depression and thought this was the way to do it.

On the day I dressed Coral in a mint-green frilly dress and a white bonnet. She looked gorgeous. I had a lovely white dress and a matching Bolero-style jacket which I had shopped for in town by myself. I wasn't having any bridesmaids due to the cost and hadn't really thought the whole wedding thing through properly. We were short of money and so Irene was brilliant. She had a posy of dried pink and white flowers made up for me and a two tier wedding cake, again which I hadn't even thought about. A spread had been laid out in the pub around the corner from the registry office for all the guests. I was still very anxious with Coral even after three months. I remember worrying when the wedding photos were being taken because I could hear her crying. My main focus was her.

Mum didn't want to come back to the pub to celebrate after we had been married but she had offered to take Coral for the night for us. I was very surprised at her offer and accepted it. Coral's things were already packed and she had everything she needed with her, so I kissed her and said goodbye reluctantly outside the registry office. It was only for one night, but it broke my heart when she went as I had never been apart from her until then. That was the moment when I realized how much I loved my little girl. Of course, that didn't make things any easier.

20. Damp

Pete and I had discussed having another baby when Coral was around six months old. It would be nice to have a little boy and our family would be complete. I didn't have to wait that long and found out I was pregnant again just before Christmas. It wasn't planned that soon ahead but nevertheless we were pleased. I was due in June again around the same time as Coral's first birthday. I was very happy about it. It just meant our plans to have another baby had been brought forward slightly.

As my pregnancy progressed so did the damp up my bedroom wall. I had been to the housing office on several occasions and complained. They kept telling me it was condensation. I was trying to be re-housed now in any case as we only had one bedroom and with the new baby coming we would cramped. On sorting through Coral's baby clothes I noticed that by the window in the bedroom the ground seemed to drop away and was lower than the rest of the floor in the room. I pulled everything out from under the chest of drawers to investigate. My mouth dropped when I found my white baby-nest covered in mill dew from the damp. My carpet was saturated. I started feeling for the areas that were wet and found the damp rot had spread across the floor and up my bed and furniture. Everything was ruined. Coral became quite ill with chest infections not long after my find. The final straw was when she was admitted to hospital with bronchiolitis from breathing in the germs.

I too was suffering from chronic chest infections. We turned the bed on its side to prevent more damage and moved the mattress and everything else out of the bedroom and in to the living room. We put the mattress on the floor in the living room and slept in there. I was bruised all over my ribs from coughing and sleeping roughly whilst heavily pregnant. Coral still had to sleep in the damp bedroom as there was no room for the cot anywhere else. The best we could do was to keep the cot as far away from the damp as possible on the other side of the bedroom. We called for a housing inspector to come and take a look. They brought in a damp meter which shot straight in to the red light as soon as contact was made with the wall leaving us in no doubt that it was definitely not condensation. They would have to move us now.

Soon after, the housing officer and another lady came to see us. We invited them in so they could see the conditions that we were living in. They had to climb over the mattress on the floor and then a coffee table before reaching the settee which was jammed up to a chair. I told them how the baby had been in hospital with bronchiolitis and was still sleeping in the damp bedroom.

"Can't the baby come in here?" she asked.

I looked around the room then back to her and said, "<u>Where?</u>"

She couldn't answer me. They offered us temporary accommodation whilst repairs were carried out in the flat and then we were expected to move back when the work was completed after six weeks. I was seven months pregnant. Were they kidding?

I said, "No way. If I'm moving, I'm moving to a house and I'm staying there."

We were offered a three bed roomed house the next day as a matter of urgency and we gladly took it.

Moving house and the stress of being pregnant must have taken its toll. Pete and I had some terrible rows, lashing out at each other. I was so scared that he would leave me that I tested him out to see if he would. I threw him out on several occasions to see if he would fight for me. One time I threw a bowl of Weetabix at him which missed and went all up the wall and stuck in the blown vinyl wallpaper.

In another argument he had hit out at me and shoved me backwards. I had been shouting at him at the top of the stairs for some reason when he lunged at me. I felt a searing pain in my ribs and I bent double in the heat of our row. For days I was in agony thinking it was all the coughing I had done. I don't doubt the coughing had weakened my chest but I couldn't sleep on my back any more, just on my left side. I was taken to hospital for an examination a few days later as I couldn't stand the pain anymore. At first they thought I was in labour until I insisted that was not the pain I was feeling. I lay back on the bed and as the doctor prodded around my ribs I bent double in agony.

"That's a cracked rib," she said without doubt.

I couldn't be bandaged up as I was pregnant and

only had another six weeks to go. I had to just endure the agony.

In mid May I decided to take Coral to Chester Zoo as a treat just for her before the baby came. I knew that I would have to divide myself between the two of them and wanted to spoil her and give her some attention on her own. I packed a large picnic of sausage rolls and egg sandwiches the way Mum made them and packed everything in a shopping trolley. I may have looked weird but I didn't care. I was eight months pregnant anyway now. We got the bus to Chester with our trolley and pram. I was quite clearly pregnant but had to stand all the way there as no one on the bus stood up and offered me a seat.

At the zoo, Coral's little face was a picture. She was so excited by all the animals. She waved her hands back and forth all day. The blood kept rushing to her head and I thought she might faint. By half past five she was so exhausted from her day out she fell asleep in her pram and we made our journey home.

I had just had my twentieth birthday and I gave birth to my son Shane at 10:16 in the morning on June 19th 1992. He had the cord wrapped around his neck and was blue at first. He was platinum blonde and a scrawny little thing. I fell in love with him in an instant. I was treated for post natal depression immediately after the birth as I had suffered it with Coral. I felt great and coped really well to begin with. It definitely helps when you know what you're doing the second time around! Coral took to her baby brother with no problems. I used to bath them together and sit them both on my knee so she could feed him his bottle. She had mothering instincts right from the beginning and was a very caring natured little girl.

At two weeks old I noticed that Shane seemed to cry a lot more than Coral had. He would wake in the night, not for anything particular but just babbled away for ages keeping us all awake. I couldn't put my finger on whether there was a problem or not at this point. He was a sickly baby too, not keeping any of his bottles down. He often projectile vomited everywhere. He was starving all the time because of this so I always seemed to be feeding him. I ended up weaning him early at eight weeks old.

In October I took a part time job in a nursing home's laundry for a few hours a day. Pete wasn't working now and we needed the money. It was hard work. the smell knocked me sick sometimes and it was a bit messy but I got on with it, until I found out I was pregnant *again*.

I had been on the pill this time, which turned out not to be suitable. I'd had a tingling sensation in my fingers which was apparently a sign of thrombosis. I had changed to a different pill but wasn't told I was not safe for the first two weeks and therefore I got caught out. I was due in July and at first I was devastated. How was I going to cope with another baby? Three of them-one after the other. I cried for days, not knowing what to do. Eventually I resigned myself to thinking there was not much that I could do but get on with it. I eventually did get used to the idea and I gave my part time job up as I was scared of slipping on the wet floor of the laundry and losing the baby. Besides, the smell of poo really was knocking me sick now!

In November I had both of my babies christened.

I wanted them to be brought up with a Christian background. I arranged the church and the christening cake which had been the top tier of our wedding cake. I had it re-iced with two bibs on the top, one pink and one blue with their names on and a tiny centre piece of pink, white and blue flowers. Coral wore a pink satin dress and Shane had on a borrowed white satin suit and matching hat that my friend Sally's little boy had worn. They were very well behaved on the day and they didn't cry at all. Afterwards we had a little celebration back at our house with friends and family. I laid on a spread and celebrated the occasion with delight.

At Christmas, I took photos of both my babies under the tree. Coral had her arm wrapped around her little brother, who could now sit up. Their flushed little faces were a picture and I clung to all the happy moments recording the photos in albums with dates and times.

With Christmas gone again I was tired, depressed and struggled with the children. Whilst I was pregnant I found it difficult to keep them occupied. They were very active and demanding children but still too young for any pre-school or nursery. I know I could have been a better mother to them. My temper was foul and I had no patience. I shouted at them a lot and I was frustrated. They deserved better. However, when I was 4½ months pregnant my baby son Shane had a serious accident which then plummeted us all in to another realm of unforeseen circumstances.

21. A Serious Accident!

It was a February morning when Shane was only 7½ months old that I got up to find his head was swollen on the left side. He seemed fine and he wasn't crying or upset, but I was worried and thought it was best to get it checked out. I didn't think for a second it was anything serious. The doctor poked around it a bit and suggested it was just a cyst or something minor and to take him to the hospital just to be on the safe side. I asked Pete if he would take him to the hospital as I had an ante-natal appointment later that morning and didn't want to miss it. Pete took Shane on the bus whilst I walked back to the doctor's again with Coral.

I was sat in the doctor's surgery when a call came through to her. She took the call then put the phone down. She turned to me and told me that the hospital had just phoned and informed her that my baby was in the hospital and had a fractured skull.

What?

I panicked.

"Oh my God!"

I hadn't heard her right. There must have been a mistake. I was totally gobsmacked. I couldn't speak or take the news in. I asked her if she was sure and how did she know. The doctor said yes she was sure, Shane had had an x-ray and did I know how it had happened.

I was totally blank and said, "No, no I don't,"

I knew what she was insinuating. I know I was having problems coping and was under a lot of strain but there was no way would I hurt my baby like that.

I stood up to go and said "I need to go to my baby, I've got to go!"

My head was in a fuzz. I became overwhelmed and sat back down, not knowing what to do. I had to take a minute to absorb what the doctor had said and then I realised from her questions what she was thinking: either myself or Pete were responsible.

I got to the hospital and Shane had been admitted to the children's ward. He appeared to be fine but only a CAT scan would tell for certain. I couldn't believe that this had happened to my baby. He had tests for brittle bone disease and all sorts of blood tests. As it was such a serious accident Social Services had to be informed and now my biggest fear was that I would get the blame. I had got the blame for everything else when I was growing up so I expected it. We were questioned profusely but we could not answer how his injury had happened. We stayed at the hospital with Shane every waking moment, worried sick. We slept and we ate there. To look at him you wouldn't have known anything was wrong, but the fear of any permanent damage had not been ruled out yet. It was a nightmare!

A few days later we were arrested and taken to the police station for questioning. Our baby needed us in the

A Serious Accident!

hospital and all anyone could do was point the finger. I understood it was procedure but even so it was awful. The police officer who questioned me suggested I had thrown my baby against a concrete wall. I was sickened by his accusations. I know these things happen but they had got it so wrong. The only explanation we could think of was that the day before his head had swollen, he had tipped sideways out of his bouncy chair and his head had hit the floor. At the time it didn't seem so serious. It was just an accident. That *had* to be how it had happened.

After a few hours of being locked up and sleeping in a police cell we were released without charge. They couldn't possibly charge us as we had done nothing wrong. We could now go back to both of our babies, but that wouldn't be the end of it.

Shane remained in the hospital for two weeks and the eventual results of his cat scan showed that he was fine and there was no permanent damage. Thank God!

We couldn't take him home, though. Social Services insisted that the children stayed at their Nan's home for the time being if she was agreeable. If she hadn't been they would have gone to foster carer's. This was the worst four months in my entire life. Even though Shane's injury was an accident they insisted we were responsible because, as the authorities said, *'He was in our care when it happened.'* We were to undergo a series of assessments and parenting skills to prove ourselves. I just felt as if they were trying to get us to admit to something we hadn't done. We were referred to a family assessment day centre for access. We saw the children daily at Irene's or the centre and tried to keep things as normal as possible for them. It was a strain on everybody. At one point after visiting the children at Irene's I was so distraught that I ran out of the house in a state thinking that I would never get my babies back home. I collapsed at a near by bus stop and cried inconsolably. I worried that the strain would affect my unborn child. I had already been diagnosed with a condition called placenta previa, meaning the baby's exit was blocked by my placenta and I may have to have a caesarean section.

The assessment centre turned out to be great. The staff there were very helpful and didn't pass judgement at all. We went there a few times a week to see the children and I personally enjoyed going. We made friends there and met other people in the same situation as us, which helped us to feel better.

Aside from eating together at the centre as a family, playing with the children and doing other activities, we also had some time in an adult group for various discussions. In one afternoon discussion Pete and I were asked how long we thought we would be together.

My reply was, *"Forever,"* and that was what I believed.

Pete's reply was, "A long time."

I will never forget another particular session in which every one was individually asked about their earliest memory, their happiest memory and their worst memory when they were growing up. The discussion got underway. It came round to my turn and I told them my earliest memory was pulling myself along the coffee table when I was a few months old, and a nappy pin pricking me by accident when my nappy was being changed. I struggled to find my happiest memory and felt like a prize idiot. There were happy memories of picnics and birthdays and things but somehow the bad memories always seemed to overshadow the good ones. My bad memories were of Mum being in hospital and me always having the blame for everything. I believed everything was my fault. I told them how Mum always told me that I had to behave or I would go in to care. How she told me I was making her ill; the constant pressure to be good. The times that she barricaded her bedroom door up and overdosed herself, or went walk about in the night whilst we slept in our beds. After the group session had ended, I was told in private I had been emotionally abused.

It was like the pieces of the jigsaw fell in to place. The proverbially penny had dropped. Emotionally abused! I would never have made this assumption myself but somehow now everything made sense. Now I had a reason for my anger and frustration all these years and I felt like a weight was lifted. I wasn't to blame for all the times I had been in and out of care. It wasn't all my fault at all. I was just a child.

My problems were not going to go away overnight, but at least this was a start. I started analysing every aspect of my life, the reasons for and the meaning of events that had taken place, the whys and wherefores. I sat with a pile of letters I had received over the years from Mum; including the one telling me I shouldn't have had a termination. I separated them all in to two piles, the good ones and the bad ones. On my left the good ones amounted to about three as I recall, usually sent when Mum was in high spirits On the right was a rather good sized handful of painful dictation. There was never a happy medium. She was either in the depths of despair or as high as a kite! I read them through one by one and cried my last cry over them. I tore the distressing ones up and swore never to keep the like of them again. Reading and re-reading them screws your brain up. I had found my own form of therapy.

In June 1993 when I was quite heavily pregnant I took my babies on holiday to Rhyl. I had already booked the holiday the year before. We were allowed to take them on the condition that Irene chaperoned us. She came with us but of course she let us go off with the children and do what we wanted to do. We stayed in a six berth caravan and had a lovely time on the beach for most of the week. I watched at my children's delight as they played in the sand with their buckets and spades. I took Coral to the water's edge to dip her feet in the waves. My huge tummy stuck out of my t-shirt as I paddled along with her. I took every moment in as they touched and watched the fish at the Sea Life Centre. Shane pressed his button nose up at the glass fish tanks in evident curiosity. We bought them ice creams and silly hats (Shane's had *'Little Rascal'* on it) and Coral rode on a bobby horse on the carousel at the fair. Pete cried as he picked her up and whirled her around the dance floor at the show bar in the evening. I could see his tears sparkle as he clung on to her. It was very emotional spending quality time with our babies after all we had all gone through. We took them swimming in the on-site pool, where Coral stood up and shouted "Mummy wee-wee!" as she peed like a horse into the pool. We couldn't help but laugh at her. It was a typical family holiday but it was special to us because we relished the time we had with our babies, just hoping that they could come home soon. The holiday was over before we knew it.

Back at home after our holiday, Shane had his first birthday and Coral had her second nine days later. I made their birthday cakes myself as Mum had used to do for Tracey and I. I iced them and decorated them with Smarties. The children lived with us for most of the time now. It was all planned out a day at a time, then more days, then weekends to gradually ease them back home.

A month later I knew I was in labour again. I was relieved that a scan had shown two weeks earlier that my placenta had moved allowing me to give birth naturally. I felt as if I had been pregnant for three years so I knew what to expect now, or at least I thought I did anyway. We were picked up that morning to go to the family centre. I guessed my labour would be a while yet as the contractions were only every hour or so. I decided I wanted to go to the centre and keep busy and moving about during the day. People thought I was joking when I said my baby would be born by tomorrow as I was having contractions. I carried on as normal throughout the day climbing over the safety gates and telephoning round to let the family know I was in labour. I was surprised and made up when it was my Mum that offered to come to our house and baby sit Coral and Shane when I went in to the hospital.

That evening I was all prepared to go. My bag was packed ready but my labour seemed to slow down and stop. Eventually I went to bed in the hope that I would get some sleep before the contractions commenced again. At two o clock in the morning I awoke suddenly. I sat bolt upright in bed and with that my waters broke. From the next room my daughter screamed out in unison with my contractions. *Very strange!!* I awoke Pete who then shot out of bed and flew down the stairs leaving me to get out of bed by myself in his blind panic. I grabbed a towel to try and catch my cascading waters (an impossible task) and followed him down the stairs to wait for the ambulance. It was as if someone had burst a huge water bomb. I sat on my towel and chatted to Mum in the mean time.

I got to the hospital and my baby had poo'd inside me. My waters were still trickling out and leaving a smelly brown trail behind me. I thought it was odd but I didn't know what it was as my waters hadn't broken in labour with the other two. It turned out he was distressed. After a few hours of labour and my legs hoisted up in stirrups-which should be made illegal!!-things did not progress and so a test was carried out. The test confirmed my baby <u>was</u> distressed and it was an emergency caesarean for me after all. I was in agony by now and so tired I felt I could not stand the pain any longer and went along with it. I remember Irene saying to me, "you've had enough haven't you love." I had.

My baby son was born on 13th July at 7.21 in the morning but he was extremely poorly. He wasn't breathing and his heart had stopped. He was resuscitated and given cardiac heart massage and spent the next week in the special care baby unit.

I was taken down from the ward to see baby *Michael* later on that day. He was a mass of tubes and wore a little white cap inside his incubator. I felt an instant rush of love and only saw my perfect baby with a mass of jet black hair asleep. We were told by a specialist doctor that

A Serious Accident!

our baby undoubtedly had cerebral palsy due to the lack of oxygen he'd received at birth. There was no knowing how long his brain had been starved of it. He would have to be closely monitored over the next year. We were told on the very same day that Coral and Shane could come home permanently. What a day!!

Michael had several fits in the first few days and I had to feed him with a syringe through a tube in his nose. I decided to express breast milk for him to give him the best start I could. I wanted to do all I could to make him well. I was able to breastfeed him properly when he was four days old as he was well enough to come out of the incubator for a feed. Nurses were amazed when he latched straight on and fed for fifteen minutes solid. The closeness and bond that I felt with Michael made me wish I had breastfed the other two. I became very overprotective of him often refusing to let people hold him as I was petrified of anything happening to him. I cuddled him constantly and didn't let him out of my sight.

A week later I was back at home with all of my children. At last I was able to bond with them <u>all</u> again and start afresh.

22. Three Babies and the To Do List

Over the next eleven months Pete and I struggled to get back to some kind of normality. Our relationship suffered greatly due to the emotional traumas we had endured and we argued a lot. It was hard going with three babies as it was let alone what we had gone through. The children were all in nappies at the same time and I now needed to potty train Coral for nursery as well as look after a newborn. Coral had been ready for potty training months ago but Pete's Mum had never got round to it. Although we were relieved to have the children back home I felt as though I'd had triplets and it was hard work. Michael had to be checked out at the hospital every three months for indications of cerebral palsy which was a constant worry, Coral was peeing everywhere and Shane's behaviour became increasingly alarming, sometimes clawing at peoples faces. Luckily we carried on going to the family centre who were very supportive to us and gave some good advice. I did mention Shane's aggressive nature to them but they seemed to think that a baby didn't have the mentality to behave that way. I felt awful for suggesting there may be a problem and I didn't bring it up again.

Michael seemed to be a doddle to care for. I hardly ever heard him he was so content. Coral and Shane played in the garden over the summer and Michael sat in his chair and sucked his dummy. In October we had Michael christened and had our usual celebratory party at our house for him.

At Christmas I made a huge effort to enjoy the festive season and make it fun for the children. I took photos of them under the tree again on Christmas eve as I have done every year since and we had a traditional Christmas dinner. I always bought them each a new suit for the big day and dressed my boys the same. People often asked if they were twins as they looked so alike. Coral always had a sparkly party dress and I would put her hair up in pretty bobbles.

I organized a huge party for boxing night and invited all our friends and family. I went to a lot of trouble. On the day my best friend Debbie and her Pete came up to help with the preparations. I worked in the kitchen all day making sandwiches, trifles and salads and cooking sausage rolls and pork pies. There was enough food to sink a battle ship. I ran upstairs to get changed hurriedly before the guests arrived. Id worked so hard and was very excited.

I was gutted when no one turned up. There had been some kind of mix up with Boxing Day not being the official Boxing Day. I don't know! It seems that people had just forgotten about it. I gave trays of food away to the neighbours so it wouldn't get wasted. It was one disaster after another. Debbie's Pete then drank far too much that night and turned nasty on us lashing out at me for no apparent reason. He hurled me to the floor in a violent outburst. Pete just stood and watched obviously not wanting to provoke him anymore. I fled up the stairs to feed Michael and stayed there petrified until they left.

This new year, after Easter I decided on some home improvements. Our living room was a large through room and we had a small kitchen. A friend of mine "Ruth" around the corner had the same shaped house as me. She had partitioned her living room off in to two rooms. I thought it was a fantastic idea. A dining room come play area for the children and a best room for us to relax in of an evening. By the summer I had put plans in to place and knocked down the existing fire place. I got rid of most of the furniture that we had to make space and pay for the improvements. I drew the plans out myself and ordered the bricks for a new fireplace which would run the length of the wall with a built in TV unit one side of the fireplace and a sideboard for my stereo the other side. We used the old bricks from the old fire place as back bricks for support and the new red bricks for the front of the new design. The plasterboards for the new wall came and Pete put the frame in. He did a good job hammering and tacking the new wall in place. It was taking shape.

One afternoon in June Pete and I got in to a huge row. It was one of those stupid rows over nothing that mattered really but the stress of having three toddlers, last years events and the fact that the house now resembled a builders yard proved too much. I had a go at him for putting too much black dye in the cement mix. Stupid I know!! It cost a fortune though and my money had run out. We argued about it and the row got so intense that I ended up telling him to pack his bags and get out. It was never meant to be a permanent thing, I'd just snapped. We needed a break and I knew he would go to Irene's for a while until things had calmed down and then come back. In the heat of the moment I had told him to take Coral with him. She was very much a daddy's girl, always clinging to him so I felt it was best. I had always thought that she hated me and didn't want me, only her Dad. I thought she would be better off with him for a few days. I would have the boys while he had her. I know now deep down she didn't hate me and at the time I thought they would be back after a few days. How wrong I turned out to be!

On my twenty second birthday…a few days later I waited for Pete and Coral to come home. I waited and I waited. It was my birthday; they had to come home today. But there was no sign of them.

I was kicking myself, oh God what have I done?

Debbie and her Pete turned up later that day and dropped the bombshell that they weren't coming home at all. They informed me that Pete had told them both I had kicked him and my daughter out. Under pressure from his Mum he had gone to a solicitor to gain custody of Coral. I went hysterical.

I was screaming inside, Hang on I didn't kick my little girl out!!

Pete and I had just had a stupid row that got out of hand and we'd all needed a break from each other. I would never have told him to take my daughter if I'd thought for one second they would not have come back home. Panic stricken I flew to the nearest public phone box to contact him. Irene answered the phone and Pete refused to speak to me. I had kicked him out before and he had always come back, but this time it was different. I phoned the police in a panic. They just told me to go and see a solicitor.

I didn't really see much of Debbie and her Pete after that. They didn't want to get involved in our domestic crisis and stayed away from me. Nine years of friendship with Debbie was gone in one fell swoop. Nor did my sister speak to me again either after that. She had started a relationship with my brother in law and as Pete's family had ostracized me I was out in the cold.

The next three weeks were a nightmare. I went down to Irene's house to get Coral and to discuss things with Pete. I tried to talk to him but I know I had hurt him too much. I desperately pleaded with him to let me take Coral back home but he refused. I had both my boys in arms and so it was impossible for me to try and take her, besides I didn't want to upset her by causing a scene. I felt intimidated by the rest of the family who were hovering about and if I'd tried to take her then things probably would have turned nasty. I took my boys back home with me and sought legal advice.

On Corals third birthday I organised a party for her. Pete at least agreed to bring her to our house for that. He was late when he arrived dressed as postman pat and most of the guests had had to leave. I had a "my little pony" cake made for her in pink icing and I bought her a play boot that opened out with little characters inside. I put the swimming pool out in the garden for them to play in as it was a gorgeous sunny day and they had a lovely time.

On the 1st of July I went to the family court with my solicitor to get my daughter back home. The judge ruled in my favour and Pete was told to return her with immediate effect. He and Irene asked through the solicitor if they could keep her till the next day. Cheek!!

I said, "No way."

They had had her for three weeks. I wanted her home as soon as possible where she belonged. It was like a scene from a movie when she was brought back home to me. I was ecstatic when she ran over the road to me with outstretched arms. I lifted her up and swung her round and then cuddled her close to me. Now I had the task of sorting out visiting arrangements and I had a brick fire place to build.

My living room was a mess. I had no carpet or settee. The partitioning wall was complete but there were stacks of bricks laid about, tools, cement trowels, bags of sand and cement and everything was black from the black cement dye. I had no choice but to get on with it. Each night when I had put my babies to bed I put on some old clothes and got to work. The first row of bricks had been laid and I had watched Pete making sausages with the cement so had an idea of how to do it. I made my mix up on a board of sand, cement and a dash of washing up liquid to smooth the mix and built my brick fire place. I carefully measured and placed each brick with a spirit level and then used a wooden yoyo to neaten it all up. It was a messy job. I sat on the front step each evening for a fag break covered in black soot. When I had finished the brick work I bought wood for the mantel pieces, sideboard and TV unit. I carefully measured and cut out the pieces with a jig saw. I sanded and varnished the wood and I mitred and trimmed decorative beading for the edges.

I had wall lights put in and I papered the walls. It took me a few weeks but I worked really hard and it kept my mind off the fact that Pete and I had split up for good. When I had finished it was beautiful and I was proud of myself. I had achieved something. Not only that but I had lost weight and had had a lot of time on my own to reflect and think.

I wasn't happy with the person I had become. At least I used to be bubbly, even with my problems. I had gradually disappeared and hadn't noticed until now. Somewhere along the line I had got totally lost and I wasn't <u>me</u> anymore. I decided on a list of things I wanted to do and set about rediscovering myself.

On my to do list was,

No 1, buy something to sit on and some carpet.

No 2, to settle the children,

No 3, to become a better parent,

No 4, to get a telephone,

No 5, to lose weight,

No 6, to go abroad,

No 7, to never wear holey knickers or my Mum's bras again,

No 8, to eventually get off benefits,

No 9, to learn to drive,

No 10, to buy a car,

No 11, to win a trophy (I didn't care what for),

No 12, to buy my own house,

During the next few weeks came the first time all three children were taken to Irene's house for access. I will never forget it. The minute Michael was put in to the car to go with his Dad; he screamed the place down for me and was very upset. Michael had only just turned one in July and we had never been apart before. I was as clingy to him as he was to me, even though I had received the good news from hospital recently that he did not have cerebral palsy after all. The specialist had jokingly called Michael a Faker and said he had escaped the condition by a fraction of a second at birth. At least now that was one less thing to worry about.

Pete did visit the children at the weekends too and I again tried to talk to him. I wanted us to give it another go and try to save our marriage but I didn't know where I stood with him. It was silly to throw five years away. I was getting mixed messages from him. He would often stay the night leading me to believe we were going to give things another try, but then he would slope off in the mornings saying he had to get back home before his Mum knew he was missing. He was my husband so why should he not stay the night? I was confused.

In September I took photos of coral on her first day at school and in October the children and I went on holiday with a friend and her daughter. Just my luck, our caravan turned out to have a gas leak and so on the third day we were moved to another caravan for safety. It was a pain humping all our stuff from one caravan to another. The weather wasn't wonderful either but we made the best of it. I played in the adventure park on the swings with the kids and my friend and I took turns in the evenings to go and play bingo, while the other one watched the children. I won some lovely champagne glasses and other things to take home. I did feel a bit rough on holiday and I couldn't help thinking that I may have been pregnant. I wasn't too much worried about it though as I thought, oh well! if I was then it would bring Pete and I back together. We would deal with this. After all we were still married.

Back home I discovered I was indeed pregnant again. It wasn't planned to have a fourth child especially given the pressure I was already under and the state of our relationship. However I was pleased about it. Unfortunately I didn't get the reaction I had hoped for. Word got round and I was told Pete wanted nothing more to do with me or my pregnancy and what's more when the child was born he was taking me to court for access. I couldn't believe it. This was straight out of the blue. There had been no particular argument and I was sure we were going to get back together or I wouldn't have let him stay over in the first place. I couldn't bring another child in to this messy situation. It wasn't fair. I already had three children that were being affected by what was happening between us. I was on my own with no money or support and I couldn't have coped with another child on my own. I didn't want to have another termination but I felt it was my only option under the circumstances. I had to put the children I already had and myself first.

My friend Sally offered to have Coral, Shane and Mike for me whilst I went to hospital in November. I would only have to be in for the afternoon. I waited in my hospital bed in the entrance to the theatre hoping that the door would burst open and Pete would rush in and shout no don't go through with it.

Wishful thinking ay!!

I kept my gaze fixed on the door. It seemed like I waited for ages. I was devastated when he didn't come and my time came to be wheeled into theatre. I went through with the termination grudgingly. Its bad enough having to do it once....But twice!! The male nurse could obviously see I was distressed and stroked my hair back telling me I would be ok. I drifted off into unconsciousness.

Afterwards the doctor who came to discharge me was quite concerned when I asked if there was a scan picture of the baby I could keep. When he had been flicking through my notes I'd noticed one between the pages that turned out to be one of the other children. I wasn't thinking clearly. Of course there wasn't a photo of a baby I wasn't going to keep. This was obviously an unusual request and the doctor did not want to discharge me until I had spoken to a health visitor or councillor. He asked me had I wanted to go through with the termination and I had said no, causing him concern. I left the hospital in a state without waiting to speak to someone and sunk in to a deep depression. I couldn't speak to anyone and I cried for weeks.

Christmas came around again. Coral was the star of Bethlehem in her school nativity play. I had helped her to make her own star hat out of a cornflake box and tin foil. I hadn't realised that they were already making stars in class. We used silver sequins and ribbon. Her star was huge and stood out against all the other children's so she led the way for all the other stars to follow. I was so proud.

On Christmas eve I took my usual photos under the tree and put the children to bed after leaving Santa a mince pie out and a glass of milk. I waited for them to fall asleep and I set about arranging their presents on the chairs and couch. I barely fitted them all into the living room. It took me hours setting everything up for the next day and I was shattered. It got quite late and when I stopped and looked at all the presents I realized how quiet it was. I was totally alone.

I wanted to tell someone look what I've got for the kids, but the silence gripped me. I had lost everything.

My best friend who I had needed so much, My Mum, my sister and Pete's family. I felt utterly alone and miserable. A tear welled up in my eye and spilled over. Then more tears followed. Then my new phone rang and Sally's drunken voice slurred,

"Hiya Gee. How do you make that snowball thing again?"

My tears turned to laughter.

God bless Sally!!

23. Enough is enough

The next few months brought me a lot of new friends and a social life. The kids were what really kept me going. I started getting out more often and this helped me enormously. I had one friend "Helen," who lived a few roads up from me and I went to her house a quite lot in the day as well as us having the odd night out. She had her hands full with five children and was single also so we had a lot in common. We used to talk for hours and have a real good laugh together. We would swap recipes and make pans of scouse for the kids' tea.

One particular day I had taken the children round to play with hers. We sat down for a cup of tea and a chat whilst they played in the back garden. She was showing me presents she had bought to put away for next Christmas and we discussed our plans for the festive season. Helen had a lovely house which was beautifully decorated and I wondered how she managed to keep sane with two more kids than I had. We stopped chatting for a minute and listened. It was quiet. Too quiet!! We realised the children must have been up to something.

On investigating we found that our little angels had opened a tin of mahogany varnish in the yard and had proceeded to paint the white patio table and chairs. Not only that but they had painted themselves from head to toe. I looked at Shane and all I could see was a dark brown head with matted brown sticky hair, a set of white teeth and the whites of his eyes peering up at me. Helen and I doubled over with laughter. It wasn't that funny later when I tried to wash it off!!!

I was also especially pally with the girl next door and started going out clubbing with her and her best friend. I had a great time out with them and really let my hair down. Thursday nights were pound a pint nights!! I always made sure the children were in bed and safe with a babysitter, but I often got far to drunk and came home far to late.

On my 23rd birthday I had a barbeque garden party and I got so drunk I ended up going down town with my slippers still on and a glass in my hand. Sometimes we would bring people back to the house and carry on the party after a night out. I had a few weekend boyfriends as I called them over the next few months. I had remained faithful to my husband for eight months after splitting up with him, but there was no chance of reconciliation now so I might as well enjoy myself. The men that I met at clubs usually turned out to be liars or cheats and so I remained single. I dabbled with substances I shouldn't have and I would be hung over all the next day when I had three children to look after.

I was going off the rails!!

I was at a club one night when Pete followed me there. It seems now I was getting on with my life without him he was interested in trying again. I had started to seek advice regarding a divorce but decided to put it on hold for the time being just in case. In July 1995 we did get back together. This was my chance and I was determined to make my marriage work. At least I would know in my mind that I had done everything I could to salvage it. I stopped going out clubbing and didn't see my friends as much anymore. My family came first. My friends weren't happy about me taking him back and they fell out with me over it. I had spent a year clubbing and partying with them and I suppose they must have felt a bit mad that I dropped everything to take him back. I just felt it was important to spend time with my husband to try and work things out. The children were made up to have us back together and that took priority. It was good at first but unfortunately all the effort seemed to be on my behalf and things became difficult again.

Now Pete was the one who went out clubbing till all hours and doing things he shouldn't have been doing. He would constantly antagonise me to cause an argument so then he would have an excuse to go out. I found the telephone numbers in his coat pocket of girls he had been sleeping with when we had been separated. I was devastated! I knew l had to put it behind me but I phoned them all one by one and asked them did they know he was still a married man at the time. One hard faced girl turned up on my doorstep wanting to know why I had phoned her house and what was it I wanted to know anyway. She admitted to sleeping with Pete several times even though he had told me it was once!! and she didn't seem to care at all that he had a wife and three children. I was embarrassed.

One day Pete went to work and didn't come back until gone two in the morning. I found out from his workmates girlfriend who had phoned me that he hadn't been to work all day. They had gone to work in the morning but had been laid off for the day so he'd gone out drinking to the pub. I had no way of contacting him. He didn't come home till two in the morning.

I decided to play it cool when he came home. He hit the roof when I <u>didn't</u> question him about his whereabouts and I told him two could play at this game. He started shouting at me and his behaviour was very intimidating. I feared what he would do so I tried to get out of the front door. I just didn't want to argue with him. He blocked my exit so I went for the window instead. This and the fact that I never saw any money from him at all signified the end of our six month reconciliation. I thought *what am I doing?* A relationship takes two and this was all one sided. I couldn't make it work by myself.

Enough was enough and I gave the go ahead for the divorce proceedings. In the mean time I tried to organise a routine for the children to visit their Dad. I felt that it was important for them to see him regularly and have contact. My efforts were fruitless and often the children were let down. Ironically Pete would sometimes turn up outside the house in the middle of the night and throw stones up at my bedroom window wanting me to let him in to stay the night. He couldn't maintain access to his children but he could manage to turn up to sleep in my bed for the night. I'd been here before.

I opened the window and shouted down to him, "go back to your mam's." I was sick of being used.

I was on my own once again and I had lost a few of my friends too since id taken him back. In fact the girl next door became a down right bully and tried to attack me one day as I came home from dropping Coral and Shane off at school. She had shouted out something not nice to me and I had said something back to her that she didn't like. She flew for me. I managed to get inside my front door and shut it behind me pushing Michael who was in front of me inside quickly before she pounced on me. Her failed attempt to clobber me angered her even more and she attempted to kick my door in whilst screaming obscenities at me. I was petrified and telephoned the police who came out and gave her a warning. On another occasion I was subject to a barrage of abuse whilst sitting watching my television. I was accused of staring out of my window at the neighbour's friend as they chatted on her doorstep. Needless to say I didn't sit near the window again for fear of a repeat of the screaming accusations.

I didn't see my friend Helen any more either as her drinking and other habits were becoming out of control. After we had drunk a bottle of wine in the afternoon one day, one of the children had got hurt. It wasn't anything serious but enough to make me realise that caring for little ones whilst even slightly intoxicated was irresponsible and stupid. Dabbling in things that were not good for me had to stop as it was affecting my daily life causing mood swings and paranoia. This was not the life I wanted. Helen didn't appreciate my new attitude and she too fell out with me.

Ruth from up the road became a close friend and a shoulder to cry on. She was a lot older and worldly wise than me and she had grown up children of her own. I would go to her house with the children when I was feeling really low and she mothered me treating me as one of her own. I even remember piling all the kids on to the pram in the middle of the night once and going round there as I was desperately upset one time. I think id had a phone call which had upset me. She was very good to me.

I started going back out at the weekends again (slightly better behaved now) with a friend from school and I found new babysitters.... a couple called, Mandy and Paul who I became good friends with. Mandy is still one of my longest and best friends.

My life settled down a little now that I was a single Mum again, even though I still had many issues to be resolved. Shane's erratic behaviour had now come to the attention of his school teachers. As far as I knew he was enjoying school and had participated in his school sports day along with his sister which I went to watch. I took photos of them both balancing on the benches and jumping through hoops. Shane also enjoyed a school trip to Camelot with his baby brother. I had them both wearing matching knitted blue cardigans. Michael was hilarious as his head bobbed back and forth on a horse ride. He looked as though he were on a real horse.

However I was called in to school one day to see the head mistress. She informed me that Shane was very aggressive and he had been known to throw pencils at his school teacher and had thrown chairs across the classroom in a temper. He was a lot to cope with at home and I had often commented that something wasn't right. I could just never put my finger on it. Now the school were noticing it too. He seemed to be going from one extreme to another. One of Shane's regular traits was to hold his breath in temper and turn blue. He would crash to the floor from lack of breath. It was extremely frightening when he did this and one time he fell cracking his head on a door frame and blacked out for a short period of time. He was hyperactive and was always tripping over his own feet and banging himself. He was so accident prone I nick named him, scar face Al Pacino.

On August 7th 1996, I moved house to a new area. I had desperately been trying for a transfer for a few months now as the victimisation and bullying I endured from the neighbours became unbearable. Every day became a chore to just walk down the path trying to avoid any contact. They had even reported me to the Social Services saying I wasn't feeding my children. The social worker who came out couldn't have timed it better. We had all just sat down at the dinner table to a huge roast chicken dinner with all the trimmings…stuffing…roasties and veg. She realised it had been malicious gossip when she saw my children tucking in and left with the knowledge that my children were well fed and well cared for. I loved my house and I still had a lot of good friends here despite the few bullies but it was time to move on. I had received a call two weeks earlier telling me a property was available and would I like to view it. It wasn't wonderful and I was sad to give up my lovely house with my beautiful fireplace but I was relieved to be going and I accepted it.

The move to my new house was the fresh start that I needed. A male friend that I had met at a club one night was a brilliant help when I moved in… even when he fixed the dado rail on upside down. He helped me out a lot and did odd jobs for me at my new place. He introduced me to his friend "Jim," who often came round with him and helped out too. I always rewarded them with their tea in return…usually a pan of scouse or bacon bone stew.

Mandy helped me to paint Coral's room in candy pink. We giggled as we painted each other in a moment of girly madness. The boys' room was painted with lush green hills, sea and blue sky on the walls. I artistically added flowers and fish to the scene I had created and painted the ceiling blue leaving white clouds behind. The children started their new school in September including my baby boy who I took photos of on his first day. They settled in with no problems.

There was a little church at the back of my new house. I felt an urge to go there as if God was saying to me, I haven't seen you for a while, come on in and visit. So I did.

It was as if I was going out of my back door and going in Gods front door. Out of my old life and into a new one.

I was welcomed in and visited the church again on several more occasions. The children were hyperactive and wouldn't sit still but no-one seemed to mind. I joined the luncheon club on a Friday and I made some nice new friends.

It was around this time that it hit me like a thunderbolt. After being bullied to move and another few unsavoury boyfriends including Pete staying the night one last time, I literally woke up one day and thought, *'What the heck have I been doing?'*

My life was a complete and utter mess and I had to do something about it.

24. A Fresh Start

My life seemed to turn around at this point. Christmas 1996 was full of the usual excitement. I attended the school nativity plays where Coral was dressed as a clown in a stripy orange and white suit and Shane was part of a human train chugging on to the stage. The beam across his bright red face was hilarious and he didn't take his eyes off me the whole time. He was so proud of himself. I splashed out on Christmas presents this year buying Coral a huge party kitchen with pots and pans. I bought Shane a workbench with working tools and Michael a red and yellow cosy coupe. I stayed up late building them on Christmas Eve. Their faces were a picture on Christmas day. That week I took them to the pantomime to see Aladdin. I was trying to make up for their Dad not being around by spoiling them. He had been such a good father when we were together and I suppose I was compensating for him not being around any more.

Access hadn't been going so well. Pete was supposed to pick them up recently for a day out and after getting them all ready in their coats and hats he didn't show up. They stood at the living room window for over an hour looking out hoping. It broke my heart to watch their disillusionment.

In the end I told them, "I don't think Daddy's coming now."

Coral refused to believe me until in the end she gave up watching for him. I took them to MacDonald's instead to try and cheer them up.

Over the last few months I had got to know Jim quite well. I remember the first time he came down my path on his bike. He did odd jobs and babysat for me a few times so I could go out with my friend. I found myself wanting to come back home to be with him. I had given up on relationships and was concentrating on the children but Jim turned out to be a good listener. I found myself able to talk to him. He seemed to understand me and I fell for his humorous personality. We used to have a cuddle on the doorstep when he left to go home. It was nice!!!

On Valentines Day in 1997 we got together. I remember the day clearly because my sister was getting married the next day to my ex brother in law. Tracey hadn't been speaking to me for a long while now. Not since I'd first split up with Pete. I had bumped into her in the market a few months before her marriage. I was in one of the stalls looking at dresses when she walked past and saw me. The weird thing was it was like looking at myself walking past. Out of the blue she shouted over to me, "Do you want to see Corals bridesmaid dress?"

I was shocked. I didn't know she was getting married, let alone my daughter be a bridesmaid for her. No one had asked me if she could be. I was going through a very messy divorce and her approach was a little insensitive.

My stunned reply was, "well I would have liked to have been asked first."

She stormed off offended by my comment and that

was the end of that. I realise now it had been her way of breaking the ice. *Hindsight is a wonderful thing!!*

I was invited to the wedding and I so wanted to go and see her on her big day. I imagined her in her white gown looking beautiful. I felt it was impossible to go. Pete's family would be there and they were now going to be my sister's family. It hurt. Debbie and her Pete would be there as they had all remained friends and Pete would be there with his new girlfriend. I couldn't take it. I wondered if I should just go and wait outside the church over the road, out of site so I could see her coming out. But I didn't!!! I didn't have the courage.

This New Year brought me several new opportunities. I wanted to find work but nothing ever seemed to fit in with the children. Leaving the children with child minders in the school holidays to go to work was not an option as Shane was so unmanageable in the daytimes. I decided to go back to college with a view to finding work in the schools. That way I could work in term time and be off when they were. I started a childcare course in the spring. I wasn't there for very long though as I was struggling to cope with the work load and home life. Michael was only in half days and Shane being such a handful was enough to contend with. His behaviour was getting worse. I caught him one day hanging out of the bedroom window shouting, "hello everyone look at me." I had to creep up behind him so as not to scare him as he may have fell, and grab him to pull him to safety.

He had stabbed his baby brother with a fork one time at the dinner table leaving prong marks in his hand. He also urinated on him, up the walls, in his workbench and in the wardrobe amongst other things. He was very aggressive and acted on impulse without thinking often kicking, punching and hitting people. Several times he was sent home from school due to his unruly behaviour. I had phoned Social Services out of desperation one day and asked for help with my son but I was basically told to get on with it. His school were helpful and referred him to a child and family organisation and a specialist doctor to discuss the matter.

By his fifth birthday my Shane was diagnosed with, *attention deficit hyperactivity disorder.* No wonder I had been up the walls with him. I felt like a weight had been lifted from my shoulders. There was reason for his challenging behaviour. Now he could get the treatment he needed. I was offered a pill called Ritalin for him. At first I was unsure about giving my child drugs to stabilise his behaviour. Ritalin is after all an amphetamine. The specialist explained how the drug does not work like that and actually helps sufferers of a.d.h.d to think before they do, and not to act on impulse. Shane was extremely impulsive and his behaviour was a constant concern. After careful thought I decided to give it a go. I had to do something or I was going to go spare and Shane was headed down a disastrous road. He was weighed and his height was measured, his blood pressure taken and he was given one tablet three times a day. I refused however to give him a fourth dose after 4pm in the evenings as in most cases, I had heard that children who take it that late end up requiring drugs to help them sleep as the Ritalin is a stimulant. In some cases I had even heard of children ending up on anti depressants because of the affect of all the medication. I didn't want that for Shane.

A Fresh Start

The medication had a significant improvement on him and helped greatly until the evening when he was usually swinging from the chandeliers again!! I thought at least if he can get him through school in the day without smacking someone I would deal with anything else at home in the evenings.

I bought a bicycle in the early part of the year with a child seat for Michael and started getting out with him in the warmer weather. We would go for rides when the other two were in school. I had been wondering why it was so difficult to ride it, until Jim laughed and pointed out that my forks and front wheel were the wrong way round. He fixed it for me as he was a cycle mechanic by trade. I would drop Michael off to school on it some days and Jim and I would go for bike rides in the woods. I had found a new interest in my bike and soon bought a newer model and began to modify it. I became quite good on it and learned to; *pull a few tricks,* as Jim said.

Pete took the children at Easter for an overnight stay. I took advantage of having no children for a weekend and went out with Jim to the local snooker hall. I met his brother and his friend Shaun and we had a great night out. I was quite good at playing pool and enjoyed the small chink of freedom I seldom got.

The children's Easter eggs were all ready for them when they came back along with a new set of clothes each as I did every year. I had laid them out carefully and looked forward to their return. I had been out the day that they were coming back home and unfortunately I was ten minutes late getting back to greet them. I had no mobile phone then to let them know. Instead of waiting for me, Pete and his girlfriend took the children back to their home. I opened my front door to find there was a crumpled note shoved through my letter box. Scrawled words telling me I would have to go to court to get the children back.

Because I was ten minutes late???

At first I thought, oh for crying out loud, but Ill be honest, I didn't panic. I knew he didn't have a cat in hell's chance of keeping my children and so I enjoyed the break making the most of it. I left it with my solicitor and put my trust in God. It did get to me seeing their Easter eggs on the side waiting for them though and I missed them.

I was in a shop in town during the three week period that he kept them from me, when Jim said to me,

"Gee, your kids are there."

I didn't hear him and shouted, "What?"

He repeated what he had said and I spun around saying, "where, where?"

By this time Pete's girlfriend was dragging them all out of the shop away from me. I hadn't seen them. They hadn't seen me either but they had seen Jim and had been shouting him. I'd heard someone's kids shouting his name but didn't register until it was too late. It all happened so fast. I could have ran after them and tried to grab one of them but what would be the point in making a big scene. I decided to do things the right way and I got my babies back home just the same.

Pete had the children for three weeks before the court ordered him to send them back home to me again. Coral told me on her return how she had been made to duck down and hide from me when they had been passing me in a taxi

After Easter I took up a challenge. An article in the local news paper had caught my eye looking for people to raise money for a charity.

On April 20th 1997 I abseiled from the Woodside ventilation tower in aid of the imperial cancer research fund. I had always wanted to abseil again after the time when I was on holiday in Llanberis. I got to do it again and raise money at the same time. I didn't raise much money but I tried. Jim, his friend Shaun and the kids came to encourage me. It was amazing. I had to go through the building and up the winding stairs first to get to the top. My legs were killing me. I came out onto the opening and it was blowing a gale. I was harnessed up and climbed over the wall at the top of the tower and with the instructor's advice I leaned back and took my first steps down the wall. I got half way down and kicked out away from the wall to drop down a little and spun around to face Liverpool. I gasped and shouted, "shiiit!!" as I overlooked the Mersey. Fabulous!

Not long after that I had to go to hospital to have a stray tooth taken out. The tooth had got lost in the roof of my mouth and was likely to cause damage to one of my good front teeth as it was resting on its root. The dentist wanted to take my wisdom teeth out whilst I was there. Although I did not want the wisdom teeth taken out as they were not bothering me in the slightest…the dentist insisted or he would not take the one in the roof of my mouth out. I had no choice. It was awful. I ended up with a huge swollen abscess on the roof of my mouth and was in so much pain it was unbearable. I could hardly speak and stopped eating. Paracetemol were not doing anything for me and I was quite ill with it. I ended up back at hospital a few days later. I was taken through to a cubicle and sat in the chair. The doctor proceeded to tilt the chair back to have a look and my head started swimming. Before I could protest I went limp and fainted in the chair with the pain. The abscess had to be cut open and drained. Sometimes I think the pain was worse than child birth! I was told not to smoke for the time being as it could cause infection in the open wounds. <u>Smoke</u>? I couldn't even eat.

That was the day that I gave up smoking for good after twelve years. I thought… if I could go without for two weeks I might as well give up altogether. I didn't even think about it. My abscess turned out to be a blessing from God in disguise!

In June I completed a twelve mile bike ride with the Wirral cycling campaign in a scheduled time of three hours. I also started taking driving lessons and I bought my first car for £150…a little gold x reg fiesta. I couldn't drive it yet but Jim could, so he Mot and taxed it so that he was able to drive it (and I could have a little practise, even when I did put it in first gear instead of reverse and hit the garden fence post!!) We did car boot sales together and took the children for days out. The car was a new lease of life for me. Jim was very good with the children too and taught Shane to ride his bike at the back of our house. Coral had her sixth birthday and Michael had his fourth. I hung balloons on the washing line for their birthday parties and made my usual home made birthday cakes for them. Their parties were never huge great affairs.

A Fresh Start

I did what I could and my lovely friend Sally would always be there with her boys. I always made my own fairy cakes and got the children to help. The licking of the spoons was a good thing that has been passed down the generations.

It was one night in the heat of the summer I decided to move house again after only a year at my present occupancy. I had never really been totally settled here. I'd never even decorated the kitchen because my heart just wasn't in it. It was an escape route from bad memories and being bullied at my last address and now I wanted to better myself. I was restless again.

The bedroom windows were wide open with the heat of summer one night and I was woken in the early hours by an argument next door but one. I stuck my head out for a nose (as you do).

Somebody's husband was not where he should have been and somebody's wife had come to fetch him. It shouldn't have been funny but Jim and I couldn't help but giggle at their antics.

We tried to contain ourselves as a voice shouted "get him out here now."

And the slurred reply was, "he wants to stay here so go home."

They were actually quite amicable but even so it's not the kind of thing you want to wake up to in the middle of the night.

I turned to Jim and said, "we've got to get out of here."

He agreed.

From Care to Somewhere

Not long after that in August I found a private property in a good area and I went for it. I needed a huge deposit but I saved the money in my determination to improve my living situation.

Our new house was huge with four bedrooms, a shower and bathroom, a sitting room, a pool room, a dining room and a massive fitted kitchen. I was able to give the boys a bedroom each which was a God send as it prevented some of the bullying poor Michael used to get from Shane. The house needed a lot of work doing to it but that didn't bother me. I got stuck in to decorating each room… Again. I knocked out the old opening in the chimney breast of the pool room to create a real fireplace. It was great hammering out the bricks and finding the old original hearth underneath. There was black soot everywhere (but I was used to that from building my old fireplace). I had the room tongue and grooved and bought a cheap pool table. Jim and I artexed the ceiling's or should I say artexed each other and we made the place our home.

We were always busy doing home improvements or bike riding or taking the kids out in the car. Life was full. We had such a laugh with each other. I have never met anyone quite so funny as him and we buzzed off each other despite some problems we'd had earlier on in our relationship.

How do I put it?

The intimate side of our relationship had suffered for some reason. I could never work out why this was and I blamed myself. This made me feel that I was unattractive to Jim and I felt that I wasn't his type. I was insecure and rattled on at him about who his type was and, what was wrong with me. It was the constant slug that chewed on my lettuce!! He always reassured me that wasn't the case but I was never quite convinced. After a rocky start to our relationship I eventually chose to ignore the problem and put it to one side. I was so happy to be in a good relationship rather than a bad one. I tried to say to myself, does it really matter? And it didn't for a while.

We settled in to our new surroundings and I felt happier here than I had ever felt in my life before. I even brought a kitten home one day to join the family and we called her Chloe.

In September we took the children to see the lights in Blackpool. It was a long drive but worth it to see their faces when we got there.

The fiesta was on its last legs so Jim had bought a new car and we regularly would pile the kids in and go for drives with the music pumping. We would got to new Brighton where they roly poly'd down the hills or we drove to Wales at the weekends. Moel Famau in Wales was a favourite place in the snow. The kids loved the trips out and at Christmas we counted Christmas trees that were lit up in people's living rooms. Sometimes our friend Shaun would follow on in his car for the fun of it. We would video our little jaunts around the country lanes. He liked to have his music pumping out too and introduced us to (ice), or, in car entertainment systems.

Another Christmas came and went and another new year dawned. Pete's access with the children had virtually dwindled to nothing. At first it was every weekend and an over night stay. Then it was one day and one night a week. Then it was one day. Then it was one day a fortnight.

One particular weekend when Jim was picking my daughter up from Pete's flat, Pete had accused Jim of dragging Shane over our pool table and throwing a snooker ball at his head. *A classic example of Chinese whispers!* In fact what had actually happened was that Michael had got in the way of a pool game being played when a ball was chipped of the table. Michael just so happened to be standing there and it flew straight at him. It was one of those you've been framed moments where everyone had howled laughing. Michael had a small round bruise but nothing serious and it was a genuine accident. No dragging of any manner had taken place! Tracey had been back in touch with me and had visited us the day it had happened with my ex brother in law. They had decided to give their own take on the incident.

The final straw was when Pete phoned to say he couldn't take the children yet again on another weekend. His reason this time being he was going to Sunday lunch at his girlfriends house. I felt he should have put his children first. He only had them once a fortnight as it was and he was letting them down again. As usual I had to pick up the pieces. When I spoke my mind about it he cut us off completely. I tried to reason with him asking him could he not take the children with him as he had prior arrangements with them. Or could he have his lunch and then have them for even an hour. I asked him to think very carefully about what his priorities were…Sunday dinner? Or your kids? That was the last the children saw of him for a relatively long period of time.

On May 7th 1998 I passed my driving test. I was thrilled given the fact that I had failed the first time around. Jim bought me a new car, a little black mg metro and this opened up a lot more opportunities for me. No one had ever given me a present that big before. I had always had an interest in cars but I hadn't realised you could actually modify them until I met Jim and Shaun. It went without saying that I was going to modify my own car starting with alloy wheels and then installing my own ice system in it.

On June 7th a month later I completed another charity bicycle ride, this time raising money for the leukaemia research. I rode thirty miles in a loop starting from Arrowe Country Park. The loop takes you right around the Wirral in a figure of eight through the country side. A friend looked after the kids in the park while we peddled away and then they welcomed us on our return three hours later. After that the leukaemia bike ride became an annual activity.

In mid June I took Shane to Chester zoo for his sixth birthday and we took Coral with Michael to green acres Farm Park a week later for her seventh birthday. She looked so adorable with her hair up in a pony tail and her peach coloured skirt and white lacy top. They enjoyed a picnic in the park area and then petted the animals. We took a tractor ride through the cow fields while the farmer told jokes and threw bread out to the animals. They fed the baby lambs and goats with bottles of warm milk provided by the farm. Michael looked so cute as he lovingly stroked a puppy. They had a lovely time. I was always trying really hard to give the children lots of good times so they would have vast happy memories. I wanted to fill their minds with good stuff like picnics and beach days and holidays so it would cloud out any bad times.

I was very happy generally but not very self confident and it still bothered me that I was not attractive enough for my partner. I was so uncomfortable with my body and It niggled at me so much I became very depressed. I started covering myself up and not wanting to go out. I hid when I got out of the bath and refused to undress in front of him. I had been to see the doctor some time ago with regards to my problem and I had been prescribed anti depressants. I was then referred to a plastic surgeon for cosmetic reasons.

An appointment came through for a consultation and at my examination it became apparent that I also had a medical condition which could have caused problems in later life. Although my stomach muscle was strong due to my vigorous workouts there was a gap in the middle from where it had stretched during pregnancy. The gap hadn't gone back to normal despite the exercise to improve it. The muscle wall holds everything in place so if not corrected eventually your insides can start to protrude out of the gap. Not good! Under the circumstances I was offered an operation to correct it. I was later booked in to hospital for an, abdomino plasty.

I was in the Chester countess for a week in July and I underwent an extremely painful procedure to repair the muscle wall in my stomach and at the same time take away the excess skin I had been left with after my caesarean section.

It was agony getting up out of my hospital bed for that first walk. I was groggy from the anaesthetic and the tears stung my eyes. I couldn't believe they made me walk so soon after. I felt like I had a giant knitting needle skewered right through my middle from hip to hip…a bit like a kebab. It especially hurt at the edges of the scars on each side of my hips. I had two drains sewn in at each side of me which collected fluid from the scar tissue. I still remember Michaels little get well picture of me in my hospital bed with two pots of blood at each side of it.

Afterwards I was bandaged up in what can only be described as a life size tubey grip which I had to wear for six weeks and I had to walk stooped over until things had settled down. Jim kept saying, "Thank you very much," as if he was the audience I was bowing too. Very funny!!! It was well worth it in the end and it did wonders for my confidence. I had a new figure and I felt great.

I hadn't been able to take Michael out on his birthday as I was still recovering from the operation. I managed to make his birthday cake and turned it in to a train using a big Swiss roll for the body, Swiss roll pieces for the wheels and chocolate squares for the windows. I also managed to complete a three day first aid course as I could be seated for the duration of it. I had given up looking for work for now as Shane was sent home from school so frequently that I would have found it impossible to juggle everything. Even if I had managed to get a job that fitted in with school hours, no doubt I would have lost it due to the many times I would be called away to fetch Shane from school or stay home with him on his many suspensions. At least passing the first aid course was something worth while.

Once I could walk about a bit more we took Michael to the bunny farm in Corwen. A fabulous little farm in Wales where I did nothing but sneeze the whole time we were there. Each time I sneezed my stomach tightened and ached. I was allergic to all the bunnies. The animals had a free reign here so the goats and ducks jumped up on you looking for food. The children were in their element. The country side was stunning and the children had another wonderful day out. Another wonderful memory!

Whilst I had been in the hospital a friend of mine that I knew from school had looked after the children for me. Jim was at work in the daytime and I would never have expected him to have them as they weren't his kids. He probably would have taken time off but I would never have asked him. My friend asked me a favour not long after I had returned home. She had enquired about becoming an Avon representative but was unable to do it for some reason. She asked me if I would like to do it and she would help me. I had known her for years so I agreed, confident that she wouldn't let me down. I pondered about it for a few days and concluded that I might as well give it a go. I'd been looking for a part time job anyway that fitted in with the children and I grasped the opportunity with both hands.

I became an Avon representative purely by chance. My friend and I did it together for a few months until eventually she got fed up with it and stopped. I had always managed the paper work and as it was in my name, I carried on serving my own customers as well as taking on hers. My little car came in handy now for dropping the orders off to her customers who lived a bit further away. I built up a round for myself and I became a successful rep very quickly. I didn't know at the time the impact that becoming an Avon representative would eventually have on me.

25. A Certificate and a Trophy

In September when the children went back to school I took up a new course as well as a parent craft class. I decided on book keeping this time. Jim, Shaun (now christened, big Shaun to save confusion between him and my son, little Shane) and I had discussed running a bicycle shop together. They were both cycle mechanics by trade and they could easily run a shop with no problem and I could learn to do the accounts. It was only an idea at this stage but I had something else to focus on. Always trying to aim a little higher. Over the next three months I went to a day college. I learned how to compile day books, operate a petty cash system and write and reconcile cash and bank records. I passed my book keeping exam with flying colours and would receive the result in the upcoming New Year.

In November my Mum fell out with me again leaving me feeling really down once more. There always seemed to be some kind of grief around Christmas. It was a pattern. I was always left broken hearted, angry with myself for letting her hurt me over and over, for letting her manipulate me. I battled inwardly having to convince myself I was not to blame. Always playing back the details to assure myself I had said the right things or done the right things. It was continuously like walking on egg shells.

She had telephoned me on this occasion to ask me what my plans were for Christmas day. I told her our plans were to stay in and have a quiet Christmas with the family. She asked me why didn't we go up to her for an hour on Christmas day but I had already made my plans.

I said, "I just want to relax this year instead of rushing around visiting and dragging the children away from their toys. It gets so stressful what with the dinner and visitors."

Mum wasn't happy. She argued, "Well you can relax when you get here. You don't have to stop long, just come up for an hour."

I offered to visit on another day such as Boxing Day or for her to spend Christmas day with us but she became quite agitated and manipulative.

When I refused to change my plans for her Mum completely lost it shouting at me, "you always do this," and hanging up.

For once it was me who remained calm. I had learned to control my temper with her.

On December 10th 1998 I entered my first, *sound off* competition which was organised by our local car accessories shop. It was a chance to get together with other people who buzzed from having loud speakers in their cars. I had enjoyed having my stereo system installed in the car and seeing what friends did with theirs. It's a whole other world. Basically a microphone is placed in to your car to measure the sound pressure level. My ice system consisted of four speakers in my parcel shelf and a sub woofer and amplifier in the boot making a pretty loud noise. I was the only girl to enter which I was proud of. I didn't come anywhere near first but I wasn't near the bottom either. I was chuffed that I had at least had a go. The car modification scene can appear to be a boy racers world but for a lot of people like me it is a reputable hobby that I am proud to say I am part of.

As part of a Christmas treat this year the children were chosen at school to go aboard, *child flight.* This is a charity run flight which flew around Liverpool for the more deserving children in the school to see Santa and his reindeer. Unfortunately at the last minute my Shane was not allowed to go due to his bad behaviour. He was considered to be a danger to himself and others around him. The school didn't want to take a chance with him on the flight because they never knew what he would do next. Although he was now receiving medication for his condition he was still hard work, very impulsive and the teachers did not want to take the risk with him on an aeroplane. Poor Shane!!

Despite Mum not speaking to me again which was nothing new anyway, we had a lovely family Christmas with the children. I took my photos under the tree again the night before and we shared our Christmas dinner together the next day. Coral played with her new doll, Shane coloured in a picture and Michael played with his new mini truck set. Michael was shattered at the end of the day and cuddled up in bed with his bunny rabbit and his new buzz light year figure. I knew I had done the right thing by staying at home for the day. I had put my children first and that was all that mattered to me.

At New Year Jim set up a little disco for the children

in the dining room. He was very musical and had a good collection of records. In his spare time he was a disc jockey and so he had all the equipment. They loved the light show and enjoyed dancing away to the music. My kids had always been very energetic and had a lot of fun with Jim. We often danced around our coffee table to the Bugsey Malone sound track. He set up a disco again in the house for our engagement party on Valentines Day 1999. I laid on a spread and our friends came to wish us well. It was a brilliant party - even when Jim's drunken brother turned up and fell in to the food table tipping it up. He lay there on top of the mounds of salads and sandwiches now on the floor and casually picked up an egg bap and tucked in. What a Muppet!!

Jim became very good at dj'ing and was soon offered work in a local night club's function suite. It was a bit of extra money and Jim was doing what he loved best. I used to go out with him now and again at weekends to the parties he was working at. I loved listening to him playing the music and sometimes got the dance floor to myself at the end of the night.

This years other events included a trip to adventure land in New Brighton at Easter, our cat Chloe having two litters of kittens that gave us all great pleasure. (We kept one of the kittens from the first litter and called him Smokey). I also changed my car and entered another sound off competition. Big Shaun won the competition for having the loudest car with the highest sound pressure level reading and my stereo system reached a reading of 130.6 decibels (something to be proud of).

After all the time and effort I had put in to making

our house a nice one, it seemed the landlord now wanted it back to sell, leaving us without a home. I was given a notice to quit after nearly two years residing here and I had no choice but to move on again. I was gutted! I had come across a little three bed roomed property in the same road where Jim's house was. I saw it and set my heart on it. Jim had lived in the road for sixteen years and so he knew most of the neighbours. It was perfect and it meant the children wouldn't have to move schools again as it was five minutes away. I telephoned the council on a daily basis asking had the keys been handed in yet. They were not aware at this point that the property had even been vacated. I was one step ahead of them. I told them I didn't care what state it was left in I would take it as it was.

As I had a notice to quit and had accumulated quite a high amount of points on a waiting list for a property, as soon as the keys did come in I was offered it immediately.

I moved once again in July 1999 and Jim officially moved in with me. As our annual holiday had already been booked prior to our move we went to Trecco bay in Wales a week later leaving the decorating until our return. It was a long drive but well worth it. The beach was absolutely fantastic and that's where we spent most of our time. We bought a dingy to ride on the waves and I helped the children to build a huge sand castle with a moat decorating it with shells for a competition that was taking place. They dug vigorously in the damp sand with much enthusiasm. I was made up when they won second place and went on to the stage in the evening show bar to receive their certificate. We spent the evenings dancing away and having a wonderful time. After the stress of moving house we had needed the break.

At Christmas 1999 another sound off competition was going to take place. I had truly got the modifying bug and set to work installing a new ice system in my car. The effort Jim and I put in was painstaking. Jim and I never ever rowed about anything but this. It had to be perfect! I couldn't stand the mess he made cutting the MDF board up for my boot build and leaving razor blades and tools lying around the house. He drove me mad. Of course we laughed about it later as we got on so well.

I designed the build in my boot which looked as if my amplifiers were sitting behind broken glass (shattered by the bass of course). I made the broken glass effect by using Perspex and adding thin lines of sticky back foil in jagged lines. I had strobe lights put in behind the Perspex and a new compact disc player built in to the boot. I screwed a sign to the wood with, IN CASE OF EMERGENCY BREAK GLASS, and I had a small fire extinguisher fitted into the boot. Nothing like a good imagination to achieve brownie points. Big Shaun welded all the gold plated speaker wire connections for my front component speakers.

Shaun and I were quite close friends by now. We often went out in the day together to car modifying shops. He used to call me, Cilla, as I was always looking for a girlfriend for him. He was a lovely man and I couldn't understand why he hadn't been snapped up years ago.

I drove in to the shop, Auto gear's car park and waited my turn to go in to the garage for the expert judge to look over my installation. I hoped that my efforts would pay off. The atmosphere was buzzing. Everyone crowded around the boot of each car as we took out turn to try and impress the judge. I chose my track from a bass cd and pressed play. The bass rumbled under me and I could see nods of approval in my rear view mirror.

At the end of the competition the winners in different categories were read out one after the other. It came to best installation and my name was called out. I had won! I was well chuffed to receive my certificate and trophy. A job well done I thought.

The owners of Auto gear were a lovely couple who we got to know quite well as our visits to the shop were very frequent. I remember using the loo one day and there was a poster up in there with a bible verse on it. I came out of the loo and said,

"Who's the Christian?"

I always knew that there was something special about, Rea. It was as if she just radiated love and kindness. When she told me that she too was a Christian I was really pleased and we both became quite emotional. Rea and her husband told us of an Alpha course that was about to start in West Kirby that had been organised by their local church in West Kirby. They asked us if we would be interested in going. I persuaded Jim to go by saying if he didn't like it he didn't have to go again and, that there was a buffet!! It transpired that he did enjoy it very much, (or at least the free food anyway!!)

The course covered many issues regarding Christianity, each week tackling a different subject. There would be a talk and then we would separate in to groups for further discussion. A spread was always laid on first and it was great to meet and eat with new people. We ended up making a lot of friends at West Kirby. I felt that I did become a stronger Christian during the course but, although I denied it at the time I also felt under a certain amount of pressure because Jim and I were, *living in sin,* so to speak. I in turn put pressure on Jim to get married because I wanted to do the right thing in the eyes of God, and to make my Mum proud of me. I loved Jim with all of my heart and I had never been so happy in all my life. Getting married made sense. My point was, we were living together anyway so what difference did it make now for us to get married? We weren't going to split up or anything!! Jim agreed with that at least and he did see things from my point of view. We talked about it for a while and eventually we set a date for September 2000.

We were going to get married.

26. The Year 2000

The year 2000 was a crazy one full of ups and downs. I had been settled at my new home for five months now. The decorating was finished and the children were happy. Initially everything had seemed fine. The couple over the road had been very friendly at first inviting us in and giving my children a packet of crisps each. I chatted to them, excited to be moving here near such nice people. Jim had known them for years as he had lived in the road a long time so we did not foresee any problems. These neighbours, Julie and Jeff warned us of certain people who were trouble makers. As it happened it was Julie, Jeff and their four children who were the ones to avoid. Little did we know the harrowing experience this awful family were to bestow upon us.

When we had first moved in July of 1999 in the middle of the summer holidays, I had told a young boy off not realising that he was Julie and Jeff's son. The boy had been standing on our fence throwing bricks over at my cat and shouting abuse to the children. When I told him to get off my fence he told me to, "eff off." Nothing major just kids being kids. However the boy went back and told his parents who then subjected me to a nasty scene in the street. It was completely uncalled for. I had been in my right to tell the boy off but Julie didn't see it like that.

She cornered me on my driveway in my car and stood

between the car door and my garden fence so I couldn't get out. She screamed fowl language and abuse at me in a drunken slur whilst jabbing her finger in my face. I didn't have a clue what it was all about at first until she pointed to the boy I had chastised and then it dawned on me. Her breath reeked of alcohol and I knew there would be no reasoning with her. It didn't finish there either. When Julie walked away still screaming obscenities, her partner then came over and had a go at me too. He was not as loud as his partner but his manner was very menacing indeed. That was only the start of our problems.

We celebrated the millennium by taking the children down to the front of the river Mersey in Birkenhead to watch the fireworks over in Liverpool. It was a spectacular display. The next day the children gathered around the huge chocolate celebration cake I had bought with 2000 piped across it for a photo. Now that the New Year was here plans for my big white wedding were underway.

The neighbours' children continued to be nuisances until in February I put a complaint in to the council. Council officers offered to go round to speak to them, and from what I gathered there had been complaints from other residents too. I didn't want the council to speak to the neighbours though as I was scared of provoking any more trouble. They would know it was me and I was scared of them. It was a catch twenty two. They gave me incident sheets to fill in recording the dates, times and the incident that had taken place. It wasn't too long before I was scribbling away.

One day I was walking up the road with my eldest

son. I saw Jeff in his front garden and I nodded and said, "hi."

I was just trying to be civil. As I got to the end of my path Jeff came over and threatened me.

He asked, "what did ya grass me up for?"

I was taken aback. I asked, "grass you up for what?"

"You grassed me up to the council. I won't tolerate that. There'll be consequences for your actions."

He poked his finger in my face at which point little Shane clung to my leg petrified. I put my hand on his head to comfort him. I quite bravely told Jeff not to threaten me in front of my seven year old son and said I had complained because his children had caused damage to my property and were abusive toward me. He leered over me.

I also said, "This is why I complained, because I couldn't knock and tell you. You are inapproachable."

I filled the sheets in for a while but then things gradually blew over. As things had calmed down I threw the incident sheets away not knowing then that I would later come to regret it. In any case, at the time I didn't really want them to get in to trouble and I felt quite guilty about reporting them.

I shouldn't have felt guilty as it wasn't long before their torrent of abuse commenced once more. Not only did they throw stones or eggs at my windows and car and bully my children threatening to take their bikes from them, but they fought amongst them selves. Their alcohol fuelled fights began to be a regular occurrence starting early on and carrying on for most of the day. If it was quiet in the day we were guaranteed a performance at three o clock in the morning. Julie's voice could be heard in her usual slurred screeching, "come ed then, bring it on, bring it on."

Or, "eff off" repeatedly.

Another favourite was, "whatever, whatever."

Their children often kicked at the front door or smashed the windows in violent out bursts. It was very funny at first and we would all go silent for a listen but it became so tiresome in the end as their arguments became more frequent and more violent. We would lie awake listening to the shenanigans in complete disbelief at their behaviour. In the middle of the summer we had to shut all our windows to block it out. Needless to say I started filling the incident sheets in again.

In June Shane turned eight and we took him to Camelot theme park for the day. The sunshine was cracking the flags and the pollen count was high. Poor Shane developed a case of, *jelly eye* as a result of hay fever and we had to hurriedly find a chemist. We managed to get the required medication and it soon settled down. We enjoyed the rides and the jousting that took place. King Arthur and his men dressed in bright colours entertained the crowds with humour and vigour.

On Corals ninth birthday we hired a huge bouncy castle and she had a barbeque garden party with all of her friends from school. I plaited her hair for her and Jim set a disco up in the garden. The children all played party games for prizes of sweets for the best dancer.

The Year 2000

At the end of August it was time for the hen and stag nights. Our wedding was fast approaching and our nights out were being recorded for sky television. My friend Mandy's Granddad worked for channel four and was organising the show. We were asked to take part with the offer of some free drinks to get the party going. I found it quite daunting having a camera and a huge microphone that resembled a big woolly sheep stuck in my face for most of the night. I had been ill for a few days prior to the night out too and wasn't feeling one hundred percent anyway. Then to top that off I went white in one of the pubs when a fireman stripper that Mandy had hired, made me lie down on the floor and bounced up and down on me in order to burst strategically placed balloons between him and myself. Call me a prude but I hated it. I had always cringed at the idea of a stripper. It just didn't do anything for me. I ran to the toilet when he had finished his act and promptly burst into tears.

The camera crew chased me into the loo to get my reaction and shouted me, "Gina are you ok?"

I wiped my tears away, stuck my head around the cubicle door with a huge grin on my face and sang out in double syllables, "ye ess." Expert at disguising emotion. I wasn't giving them the satisfaction of my tears for audience ratings. The girls told me not to worry as Jim was going to a lap dancing bar anyway. Oh was he now! I was relieved that he was getting the same treatment as me. It made me feel better but I was shocked that he hadn't mentioned it for more than two weeks. Well hadn't mentioned at all is more precise. He knew I had strong feelings about certain after hours activities shall we say and so he had kept it a secret. I felt a bit deceived if I'm being honest. After I had brushed my hair in the mirror and applied some more lipstick we went over to Liverpool in a limousine and I danced the night away. I didn't drink too much because my stomach still wasn't quite back to normal from the bug I'd had.

The next day the television crew came to finish off recording for the programme. It was fun at first as they filmed our modified cars and ice systems because that was a big part of our lives. Seven hours later and no break I was well cheesed off. I wanted them to just go away and leave us alone. They asked a lot of questions about how we met and our engagement. They tried to put words in my mouth and to get me to say things that I didn't believe in or didn't agree with. I was encouraged to portray myself as a Christian gone wrong because Jim and I lived together before marriage and I refused. They invited me to shrug it off as if I believed it, but just didn't care anyway. I did care. I was not a Christian gone wrong, just a normal person who makes mistakes the same as everyone else. God can guide us to do the right things but it is up to us to make the right choices.

As I watched Jim being filmed and the things he was coming out with, I started wondering if I really knew him at all. He seemed to lap up the encouragement and I was surprised at his responsiveness to the film crew. The whole weekend made Jim come across to me like a different person. It made me question if the reason we had problems in our intimate life was because he was suppressing himself self knowing that I may be offended by his desires. He was hiding what he really wanted because of me. He had hidden the fact that he was visiting a lap dancing club knowing I would have disagreed with it. By hiding it I felt that he must have wanted to go, or he would have objected to it. My mind was a whirl. So many questions were now racing through my head. Was I doing the right thing? These doubts stayed with me for the next two weeks.

There were a few times in the lead up to the wedding when I had become quite dizzy and light headed and I would have to sit down. The week before I got married Mandy who was to be my chief bridesmaid was doing a practice run on my hair and I had felt faint then. She made me a glass of juice and I was alright after a drink and a sit down. I shrugged it off and thought no more of it. Probably just wedding nerves. Aside from that I had enjoyed every second of planning my wedding and I hadn't stressed out about it at all.

Before I knew it September was here and my wedding day had arrived. It came around so quickly. It was organised chaos at my house. Everyone was bustling about tripping over each other. I will never forget the bouquets arriving as we were all getting ready. The aroma of freshly cut crimson and white roses drifted up the stairs and filled the air with fresh sweetness. By now I had lost a lot of weight so my dress fitted me perfectly, if anything it was slightly too big now. I had been going to a gym three times a week to get trim but the weight was just falling off me now.

It was a traditional white gown with intricately, heavy sequined and beaded design. It had a three foot train and was off the shoulder with a little cap sleeve. The fitted bodice style top was heavily beaded and sequined with a sweet heart neck line and came out full from underneath the bust. I wore a hoop underneath to give it a full skirt and I had crimson coloured sparkly shoes. *Very me!!!* I opted for elbow length satin gloves a diamante tiara and veil and I felt like a princess.

Half way to the church I realised I had forgotten my veil and the limousine had to turn back home to go and get it. The neighbours must have thought I'd changed my mind when they saw the vehicle coming back up the road!! Ruth ran inside to get it for me and we set off for the church once more. The driver was in such a rush as we were late now. He sped along to try an gain some time whilst Ruth helped me to adjust my veil to my hair. We were halfway to the church when suddenly a car braked harshly in front of us and the driver had to brake in unison to stop from slamming into the back of it. The limo swerved sideways and screeched to a halt. The smell of burning rubber filled the air and I whooped in excitement. The driver was very apologetic although he shouldn't have worried… he'd made my day. No one got hurt.

I had five bridesmaids in all including my daughter. I had set her hair in curlers the night before so it was in spirals. They all wore matching gold dresses, the two little ones in tutu style ones and they all had matching pearl tiaras. *So cute!!* My boys were in little suits too with waistcoats and cravat's that matched the material of the dresses.

I arrived at the church in the white limousine with Ruth who I had asked to give me away. She had been so good to me over the years that she was definitely the right choice. She was my substitute Mum. She had made the bridesmaids dresses herself and organised a posh buffet for our reception. She even went the whole hog and wore the tails along with the best man and my boys.

The church was adorned with two huge floral bouquets to match mine and the bridesmaids. As I walked down the aisle I remember stopping at every other pew and saying, "hiya!!" to the guests. It felt rude not to say hello. The church was full of friends from the alpha course and Jims family. Big Shaun wasn't there as he hadn't really spoken to us for the last ten months since we'd announced our plans to get wed. My Mum was there but my sister wasn't speaking to me again so she didn't go either. I took in every second of the day and I honestly meant every word I said to Jim. All my previous doubts seemed to disappear and I believed that any problems in our private life would resolve themselves now we were married. I trusted in God and I was blissfully happy. We honeymooned for a week at Jim's brother's house in London, visiting Windsor castle and Big Ben during our stay.

Two weeks later and back at home our lives were about to be turned upside down. It seems our nasty neighbours had got wind of the incident sheets we, and other people were filling in.

We could hear a fracas emanating from outside our house one evening and Julie's voice shouting, "you better sort it out now, get her out here."

Jeff knocked on our door.

I went stiff and said to Jim, "don't let him in."

Jim had known Jeff for years and so he thought he would be able to talk to him. Despite my request he let him in. I was in the middle of filling in an incident sheet when he drifted past me. The stench of ale filled my living room.

He said, "what's goin on then, what's all this about a petition?"

Uncomfortably I replied holding the sheets up, "What petition? I'm filling in these incident sheets because I'm sick of your kids bullying my kids and throwing stones at the windows. There is no petition."

He answered, "well if you come and see me ill sort them out."

I was amazed. He was oblivious to the fact that he had threatened me months earlier and at how intimidating he and his family were.

I was physically shaking but I told him, "I can't come to see you as you are unapproachable and you have threatened me once before."

With that there came banging on our front door and Julie demanding we let her in. The house was surrounded by her, her four teenage children and all their friends.

Even Jeff said, "don't let her in, she's pissed."

I asked Jim, "don't let her in." But stupidly he did.

Immediately she became abusive screaming at me.

I said to her, "don't shout at me in my house please, this is why I've complained because I can't talk to you, you are unapproachable. Look at yourself."

She carried on and it was clear I wasn't going to get anywhere. She screeched several disgusting names at me before I ran upstairs to phone the police. My children who had been bullied up the stairs by her when she came in, were now all hysterical and crying. My son had nearly wet himself with fright. I cuddled them all close and told them not to worry.

I could hear Julie ranting, "Get her down here now," through the floor before she came to the bottom of the stairs and shouted for me to come down. I leaned over the banister and refused as she was being abusive.

I looked down my stairs and said, "I've got three frightened children up here now. I've phoned the police, I don't know what you want to do about it but I've phoned them and they're on the way."

With that she left screaming at me, "ooohh that's right phone the police ya effing grass" as she went.

I could hear her daughter shouting, "I'm gonna knock her effing head off and put it on a stick" as she furiously booted at my door in an attempt to break it down. A half full can of beer was hurled up at the bedroom window smashing it before bouncing off and landing on my car. Bricks and stones were thrown at the windows from all sides and abuse rained on us. It was terrifying.

The police arrived and a statement was taken. Of course they had gone quiet now. The officer went over to warn the family to stay away from us. He came back over to us and said Jeff had gone out in his car so he hadn't been able to warn him, but he had spoken to Julie and found her to be abusive and incoherent. He had given her a warning and was confident he had dealt with the situation and left our property. He told us he would be back tomorrow to warn Jeff as well. I resigned myself to the kitchen which was at the back of the house and away from any more oncoming abuse. Coral went in to sleep with her brothers also at the back of the house as she was so scared.

It was twenty minutes or so later when we heard several sirens along the main road.

I commented to Jim "oooohh God something's going on somewhere."

I was unaware that they were speeding back up this way to an emergency call from over the road. The officer that had left our property got back to his car just as Jeff was returning in his car. The officer went over to their house again to warn him to leave us alone. He had then entered their property and was assaulted from behind and knocked to the ground. He had called for back up which arrived and chaos had ensued. On peeping out of our bedroom window it looked like the whole road was under siege. The whole family were in the street shouting and screaming. Julie attacked a police woman that had arrived on the scene so she was arrested and carted off along with Jeff. He was charged with affray and our lives were made even more of a misery from then on.

This was the point when the Anti social behaviour team, or neighbour hood nuisance team as it was called then, became involved. They offered to set up CCTV and a full working alarm system. We bought security lights and I took to keeping my windows shut at all times. Before I went out anywhere I checked the coast was clear first and jumped in to my car locking myself in for fear of being attacked. I even delivered my Avon orders to customers in the street in my car. I refused to walk anywhere.

At the beginning of October another incident took place which spurred me on to go ahead with the surveillance cameras I had been offered. I was sat on my bed in the dark watching out of the window. The whole thing had taken over my life and I was constantly watching out in case they did something. I sat motionless on guard on my bed and watched Jeff come out of his house with his oldest son. It was dark out but the orange glowing street lamp at the bottom of my driveway made them visible. The father crouched down behind my front garden fence. I could see him glancing around the fence obviously checking to see if anyone was watching him. He couldn't see me sitting in the dark in my bedroom. He then swiftly jumped up, threw his jacket over his head, crouched down again and scuffled over to my car. Before I could protest I had gone rigid with fear. He raised what looked like a screw driver and began stabbing at my tires. When he had finished he casually waltzed down my drive, stood up and went back up his own path in to his house. I could have shouted out but I was petrified of what else they might do.

I was gob smacked!! I panicked and immediately telephoned the police and relayed to them what I had just witnessed. I took Jeff to court but his mother lied for him stating that he had been at her house during the incident so it couldn't have been him. He got away with it leaving me totally deflated. It was as if they were untouchable.

Just two weeks before bonfire night would be the night we caught crucial evidence on camera. I was consumed with fear and my insides twisted at the notion of catching them doing something that could be used as evidence against them. We were sat in our living room and a loud crack hit our window. A lit firework had been thrown bouncing off the window and then exploded on to my car setting the alarm off. Then as I looked out of the window another loud crack and I ducked as a second firework bounced off the pane. We vacated our living room in a blind panic and phoned the police.

Twenty seven fireworks in all were launched towards our house that night causing damage to both our cars. Jim went in to the back garden and looked over the fence to see where they were coming from and a firework landed on his feet. He reported back that Jeff and his kids were standing on top of our next door neighbours' car, lighting the fireworks in their hands and throwing them directly at us. I wouldn't have believed it if I hadn't seen it with my own eyes. I'd loved bonfire night up until now. Now I hate it as it is a terrible reminder of what we went through. The police came out and walked up the road a few times but as the neighbours kept the fireworks inside their house they were powerless to do anything. They could only do anything if the neighbours were caught actually throwing them but of course they made sure the police had gone before lighting their next weapon.

We were offered temporary accommodation that night by the anti social behaviour team but I declined. I was too scared to leave my house in case they vandalised it or worse and I was scared to stay. We couldn't win!!

We went out to a friend's house on bonfire night just in case there was a repeat performance. I didn't even want to do bonfire night now and was very emotional.

The Year 2000

We came back to two windows smashed at the side of the house. In all, my daughter's window was broken five times leaving glass shattered on her bed and all over her toys. It had to eventually be replaced with a temporary Perspex window.

By Christmas I was becoming quite ill. My next door neighbour (who was also targeted for complaining and whose car had been used as the firework launching station) and I sent our Christmas cards to each other in the post because we were too scared to walk up the others path. My weight had plummeted to eight stone and six pounds. My hair was falling out and left me with a bald patch at the front of my head, I was depressed not wanting to go out or get up and dressed in the morning. I couldn't sleep and I was a nervous wreck. I went to the doctor who prescribed me anti depressants. I didn't really want to take that route because of my Mum's history but I needed the help and I took them.

Why suffer if you don't have to.

Mum spent Christmas day with us this year and we still managed to have a good time despite the conflict with our neighbours.

The New Year 2001 brought crisp white snow with it. Our garden looked like a fairy tale scene draped in its silent icy blanket.

Silent until my kids got out there for a snowball fight anyway!!!

At least at the back of our house we were out of sight of any trouble brewing. I was not sad to see the back of the year 2000 and its troubles.

27. Eviction

Jim had been telling me to go to the doctors again but I just kept shrugging it off. By Easter the dizzy spells and faintness had worsened. My cheek bones were protruding and I was looking gaunt and pale. It came to the point when I knew something was wrong. Losing my hair was the worst thing and that was the final straw. Every time I pulled the brush through my hair thick wads of blonde would be left behind in the bristles thinning me even more. The weight was still falling off me even when I was eating chocolate and chips!! I was starving all the time and waking in the middle of the night absolutely ravenous. Other times I would wake grinding my teeth together or having nightmares of teeth falling out or teeth hanging from my mouth on a thin bit of bloody gum. I was shaking and out of breath a lot, even just walking down the road but I couldn't keep still. My mind was constantly alert. I would sip juice to make myself feel better and I thought I may have been diabetic. I made an appointment and went along to see my GP.

He monitored my heart rate and said, "mmmm, I don't think your diabetic but we do need to run some tests."

My heart was speeding along at 114 bpm….sitting down….doing nothing. He said it was quite fast but told me not to worry. I had blood taken and a few days later

Eviction

I received a call asking me to go in to the surgery. I was diagnosed with, *hyperthyroidism* or *graves disease*. This revelation explained the weight loss, dizziness, depression and lack of sleep. I was referred to a specialist for treatment and over the next few years my thyroid would be up and down like a yoyo. Although my Mum has the condition and it is said to be hereditary, it is also thought that stress can actually trigger it off. I was one hundred percent positive that the torment I had suffered over the last year was key. However our ordeal was not yet over.

I had relayed my problematic thyroid and our troublesome neighbours to Rea. My mind just couldn't relax. She was very comforting and gave me a card with a verse on. *'Be still, and know that I am God, Psalm 46:10.'* This helped me a great deal.

We were sitting in our living room again one night when I heard a loud bang and my car alarm instantaneously sounded. I jumped up and ran outside to see what it was. At the back of my car lay a red brick and a huge dint in the rear panel of my car indicated to me that the brick had made contact there. *I was so angry.* I went upstairs and rewound the cassette that had been recording on our surveillance monitor. I was horrified to watch Jeff's oldest son come up the road with a loose brick taken from another neighbour's garden wall. I watched him take it and hide it beneath his jacket. He then walked up to the end of our driveway. He looked all around to check no one was watching and then he launched the brick straight at the back of my car and ran.

Another incident recorded included the family setting fire to their own car. Not knowing the whole thing was on tape they tried to have <u>me</u> charged with arson claiming I had done it. Muppets!

By now enough evidence had gathered and it was decided to apply to court for an eviction notice to be served on the family. I had never wanted them to lose their home but at the end of the day it was either them or me. I had been bullied before and had moved house because of it. No way was I doing it again. The bullying I endured here was ten times worse and someone had to do something about it. If I moved they would only bully the next person that came along.

There were seven of us altogether that went to court in June 2001 to testify. We thought this would be it, an end to our misery and we could all move on with our lives. I was petrified of seeing any of them in the waiting area. I needn't have worried, as they didn't turn up. Julie claimed she was too ill (intoxicated more like!!) and court was adjourned. I couldn't believe it. I wanted to give up on the whole thing and felt I couldn't cope anymore. We would have to tolerate abuse for a further three months now. My next door neighbour was in a tearful state like me. We hugged and encouraged each other to go on. On the plus side Jeff's court case regarding the charge of affray soon arrived and he was found guilty. He was convicted and sentenced to four months at her majesty's pleasure. This at least gave us a glimmer of hope.

In July we all went to the max power live show in Birmingham together with a few other people. The cars were amazing and the stereos were hoofing!! I had bought a new car in January but had kept it hidden at Jim's auntie's house so it didn't get smashed up by the neighbours. I had got the modifying bug again and had plans for my new, *rocket* as I called it. I had already bought an alloy gear knob, pedals, fuel cap, wheels and steering wheel. I had a huge spoiler fitted to the rear and a front grille. It was printed in "fast car" magazine on the readers rides page. I was well made up.

On the 25th August 2001 I took the family on holiday to Cornwall, legendary birthplace of King Arthur. I have always been fascinated with castles and archaeology and I was in my element to come here. Besides we needed the holiday after all the stress and it did us the world of good. We woke up in the early hours to make a head start and I drove most of the way which took a good nine hours.

The sea waters were crystal clear and the beach was a haven of rock pools. The huge waves crashed over your head and beckoned to the many surfers we saw there. To reach the beach, at the back of our caravan we had to walk down a sand bank that was so steep you could barely stand upright. It was fun running down it but a hike going back up it. The children played with their vortex ball which whizzed through the air, and they buried each other in the sand. My Shane ever the joker of the family buried himself and made a pair of sand boobs on himself. Very funny.

I took the children to nearby attractions, miniature world one day and, farm world another where they got to milk, Clarabelle the cyber cow .We walked around the farms lake which was home to two swans, Arthur and Guinevere, and surplus amounts of fish. Jim and I delighted ourselves with lunches of traditional Cornish pasties and the cream teas on offer. I have never seen

Cornish pasties like it. They were the size of an elephant's foot. We visited the Cornish goldsmiths and, *Cornish pearl,* where my daughter and I picked our own oysters from a huge glass tank. They were then opened in front of us to reveal the pearl inside which was then authenticated. Coral's was a pink pearl which I would keep for her till she was old enough to have it and mine was a gold one. As we are both born in June, pearls are our birth stone. Something that just her and I shared that day.

Another trip out was by a steam train, the only way you could reach the, *Lappa valley.* The Lappa valley was home to an old engine house which told the tragic story of a wild flood a long time ago where many of the workers had drowned.

The high light of the holiday for me was on the last day when we visited Tintagel castle on the way home. As soon as the headland came in to view I was breathless. Craggy rocks and steep stone stair cases plunging down toward the crashing waves. A modern wooden stair case now carries you across from the mainland to the island where the legendary, *Igraine* was kept hidden away. Her beauty was said to be so captivating that every man wanted to make her theirs. The beautiful ruins of such a magnificent place sadly eroded into the harsh cutting sea. Courtyards and latrines can still be seen along with a chapel and an ancient garden. What remains can only invoke the imagination. It was a case of reality bites when back home after our holiday.

The neighbours now knew that we had surveillance cameras fitted and they played up to them. Even knowing that they were there still wasn't enough for them to kerb their atrocities. Jeff stood out in the road one day looking up exactly where one of the cameras were hidden. He beckoned with his arms held out and shouted, "Come on then, out here now."

Another time they had all come past the house shouting and being abusive toward somebody else in the neighbourhood. I believed they had all been to the local park to beat a foreign exchange student up for some reason.

He pointed up to the camera and hissed, "pisser!"

The day of the court case had arrived and I was a bag of nerves. It was September 13th 2001. We waited in anticipation for Julie's arrival but once again she didn't show up claiming poor health was to blame for her non appearance. This time the case went ahead without her and the judge ruled in our favour. Our nasty neighbours were given twenty eight days to vacate the property leaving us gasping with relief. It was finally over. Thank God!!

The local news papers read like this:

Family from hell faces eviction

A WIRRAL MOTHER-OF-FOUR whose family terrorised their neighbours for two years has been given 28 days to get out of her council house.

A judge at Liverpool county court granted an application by Wirral council for possession of her house, after hearing how the "neighbours from hell" turned the quiet cul-de-sac into a war zone for other residents, one of whom had fireworks aimed at her house and her car damaged by bricks.

The woman, who is in her early forties, was not present at the hearing because of health problems, but her failure to comply with previous court orders stopped her and any witnesses she may have wanted to call from giving evidence.

Her partner who is forty nine years old, is serving four months following a conviction for affray in August.

The judge, who rejected an adjournment application, heard from seven neighbours and council officers, including the manager of the neighbour nuisance team before deciding in favour of eviction.

The judge said that the council claimed the defendant was in breach of her tenancy agreement, which prevents the tenant behaving in a way which causes nuisance and harassment.

"Residents have been subjected to a barrage of abuse, loud noise and vindictive actions from the defendant and her family. The children seemed to have been allowed to run rampant. There appears to have been no restraint or proper parental guidance."

"Officials have attempted to reason with her but she has adamantly refused to listen. It's time to say enough is enough."

Afterwards the manager of the neighbour nuisance team said she was duty bound to help them find somewhere to live but they would not be offered a council home.

The court heard that mother of three Gina Worrall who lives next door but one to the defendant is suffering from chronic anxiety and depression which with continued harassment could lead to a complete nervous breakdown.

After the hearing she said "it's been a living nightmare, two years of hell. Two weeks before bonfire night 27 rockets were bounced off my windows from their driveway. We were frightened they would come through the window."

Mrs Worrall said she wanted to dispel a belief held by the defendant that she had organised a petition.

"She came in to my house accusing me of all kinds, of spying on her and going around the neighbours. All we wanted was for them to leave us alone. There was no way I was moving out of my house.

She added that events had triggered a hyperactive thyroid condition which will be with her for the rest of her life.

Courtesy of the Wirral Globe.

The family went into self destruct mode after that. There wasn't a fence panel left intact or a window left unbroken at the front of their house. People walking past thought the family had already vacated the property as the windows were all boarded up.

One night before their departure a row ensued late on in the evening. Julie came out in a very thin nighty and not much else, arguing with her son over a garden brush. After he had thrown it at her, she picked it up and turned to go back inside the house when he ran at her from behind. It seemed as if it was in slow motion when he pushed her in the middle of her back hard and sent her flying forwards, arms outstretched like a bird. She landed flat on her face on the ground.

It was a disgrace. Fancy doing that to your Mum! Well there was just no respect for anyone, not even each other.

The day they left I felt like I had won the battle, but I couldn't help feeling sorry for Julie. The family had desperately needed help, but then again maybe they were beyond it. The way I saw it was, I had put my children and family first. Now we could move on with our lives. A huge white sign was hung on the now tranquil house stating that the family had been evicted due to their anti social behaviour. A stark warning to other would be nuisances that there are consequences for their actions.

I am still haunted by loud noises, fireworks and bangs to this day. If I hear anything outside I am straight up to my living room window to check. Some things like that just stay with you forever.

If anything my experience has taught me one thing. People should have respect for one another. Sadly this is not always the case though. It is a scary thing to have to stand up for your self sometimes, but this kind of behaviour should not ever be tolerated. The help and support is out there, you just need to be brave and take it. I could have just given up and moved house because of them, but that meant they would have won. They would only have persecuted the next person to move in to our house. I believe that our communities should all work together and fight together to eradicate anti social behaviour once and for all.

28. Ibiza

Our street was blissfully silent, almost eerie at times. Jim and I had finally settled in to married life and my Avon round was becoming very successful. The children and I had become regulars at the local chapel near by and I had made some good friends over the last year. I had helped out with one of the church luncheon club's meals, making an apple crumble and I felt like I belonged there. The children attended the Sunday school and they all had a part in the nativity play which I went to see. Life was good.

One of the happiest Christmases I can ever recall was that of 2001. My sister and I had been in contact now quite regularly and we were closer than we had ever been before. She came to my house weekly and Jim would give her a lift home later on in the evening. We had a great night out in December, dressing up all glitzy and glamorous for the occasion. She wore a long shimmering red dress whilst I wore a leopard print halter neck number with an asymmetric hemline. We straightened our hair and sprayed some shine spray on. Things had been up and down with us in the past but I hoped now that any problems that may arise would be dealt with without everyone falling out. It had never been my bag to not speak to someone. If issues needed resolving isn't it better to talk about them?

Tracey had long since split up with her husband (my ex brother in law). She had been in another relationship since him and that had ended also. She had been trying for a baby for a while with him before they had split up. Sadly for her it just never happened. After treatment to help her produce eggs and no results she had given up. At twenty eight her hopes of becoming a mother had been dashed. She just learned to live with it.

Mum and I were getting on great for a change at this point and I was confident that we would never fall out again. I trusted God and seemed to be able to cope with her and avoided confrontation the best I could. For the first time in a long time we all spent Christmas day together. It was as if all my prayers had been answered. We all sat around the table for our Christmas dinner donning the daft paper hats, pulled our crackers and lit the festive candles. We laughed and joked and all huddled up together for a family photo. After we had eaten we all fell on to the sofa in a gelatinous heap, full of Christmas pudding to watch the TV, whilst the children played with their new toys. It was magic when we looked out of the window and it was snowing! Wow!

Tracey and I chatted in the New Year and decided to go abroad in the summer along with a friend of mine. The children were going camping for a week so I thought I may as well make the most of my freedom. It was something I had always wanted to do and now I had the opportunity I was going to grab it with two hands. Jim didn't want to go abroad as he couldn't stand the heat and was scared of flying so it was going to be a girly week away. The original intention was to go to Aiya Napa in Cyprus or somewhere further but Tracey ummd and ahhhd. She fretted about how much money it was going to cost and what she could afford. We came to a compromise to satisfy everyone.

We made a booking to go to san Antonio bay, Ibiza in June that year. That's when the apple cart tipped over.

Tracey then started panicking about me and my friend leaving her on her own on the trip. She obsessed that we may fall out with each other, or she may get ill as she suffered with, *Chrones disease.* It seemed like she was looking for problems and her erratic behaviour mirrored my Mum's .Then there was a misunderstanding over sleeping arrangements and things got out of hand. I can honestly say that I really did my utmost to resolve the situation. I constantly tried to reassure my sister that the holiday was about enjoying ourselves and having a good time. I tried to get her to be positive instead of negative. I know in some cases things can go wrong but you cant live your life treading on egg shells. I promised her any problems would be dealt with should they arise. I just wanted her to get excited like me and shout, "YAY were going to Ibiza." Even my Mum says Tracey can be stubborn at times and, my gosh, she really was!!

By March only Tracey's payment remained to be made. I was frustrated when she refused to speak to me and would not answer her phone. I didn't know what to do. My friend was stuck in the middle and feeling awkward about the whole situation. We had paid our money in full but if Tracey didn't make her payment we would lose the whole holiday. Our only other option was to either pay hers for her, or cancel her off the holiday completely, meaning she would lose her one hundred pound deposit. I didn't want to cancel her off but I couldn't afford to pay her share either. I telephoned her on several occasions and made a desperate last attempt to pacify her by visiting her at her flat. I talked and talked with her for hours. She had an answer for everything and her fears were too great for me to conquer. I felt drained. I had to pick the children up from school eventually so I left the flat leaving her the option to meet up again a few days later to discuss the matter. I left her with the date by which the payment was to be made. I really couldn't do anymore than I had.

Sadly she didn't contact me or make the payment. We had no choice but to cancel her from the holiday. I knew she probably wouldn't speak to me again after that...... and she didn't for another two and a half years.

Mum got involved too and she fell out with me taking sides. I was accused of using my sons disability allowance to pay to go to Ibiza, and of stealing the one hundred pound deposit that my sister had now lost as a result of the cancellation. My Mum threatened to take court action against me and wrote me a letter saying how selfish I was to take much needed money from my sister's pocket. I had to go to the travel agent to get a copy of the documents to prove to her that I hadn't taken it. The travel agent was completely astonished at my request. I felt embarrassed that my family thought so little of me. All this over a holiday!

I was disheartened at these latest events, as I had trusted in God and believed our relationship was at last healing. I battled with my faith at this point and wondered why my Mum could never see the good in me.

I travelled with my friend to Ibiza on June 2nd 2002. (Paid for with my, Avon earnings!) I had never flown

Ibiza

before and I couldn't wait. We were staying in a brand new pristine white hotel in San Antonio bay.

On our first night there we took a trip out on a cruiser around the bay and supped the local tipple of sangria. The cliffs towered high above us in majestic splendour as we sailed past. It was a little overcast that night so we didn't really get to see the sun setting in all her Spanish glory. Apparently it was a sight to behold. We were dropped off in the centre of San Antonio where our hotel rep showed us around giving us a taste of the local night life.

The views across the beautiful turquoise bay from our hotel were of little white buildings in the distance dotted around the coastline. I was amazed by the sight of grapes growing freely on the vines and the geckoes hopping about in the grass. We visited a walled town and castle where from the top the views were spectacular. We shopped in the town and lay by our hotel pool basking in the sun. We sampled the local dishes and cocktails. I think I gained half a stone drinking, coco locos

A very good night out we had was at a karaoke bar which was half way around the bay. We'd stopped off there with two girls we had met at our hotel for a jug of cocktail, and ended up playing pool with a group of lads from our own home town. I then jumped up with one of the girls on to the mini stage and we belted out the song, *I'm so excited,* over the microphone. My first time doing karaoke and I loved it.

We took a trip out another day by boat to, *Cala Bassa* which was a tiny palm fringed bay you could only reach by boat. The sea was really choppy that day and the icy wind tore through my hair. I had picked up a few

Spanish words and thought it was hilarious repeating *"Es pellegrosse!"* It may have been a bumpy, uncomfortable trip but I was so happy and absorbed in any new experience. I had waited a lifetime to get here.

At the bay it was warm and inviting. Nothing like the trip to get there. The fish could be clearly seen swimming around your legs in the transparent tepid waters here. I went for a dip then I lay back on my sun bed and soaked the sun up whilst the shallow waves lapped against the shore in front of me. My friend opened a can of olives for us to nibble on. Perfect!!

On our last night we went to a water party in a club called, *Es Paradis,* one of Ibiza's big clubs. We had waited all week for our big night out and dressed up for the occasion. We went out late which is the done thing over there as the clubs open early in the morning. My first impression of the club was that it looked like a shopping centre. White shiny buffed floors and grand looking staircases with plants twisted around them. It was huge!

In the centre of the club was a round section that descended beneath the floor level. It reminded me of a small amphitheatre with stone steps all the way around it and the dance floor was at the bottom. A small dance cage was suspended above the dance floor in mid air. Scatter cushions lay on the steps for your comfort giving a very lush appearance. We danced until five in the morning willing the water to appear. We were starving by this time and I chewed the wedge of lemon in my drink with great satisfaction. When at last the water appeared the whole club erupted with life. The dance floor filled up like a swimming pool with water jetting out from the steps. It was amazing.

We did get to see the sun setting before we left Ibiza. We sat eating paella in a local taverna and watched it dip between the cliffs either side of the bay, lower and lower like a huge golden penny in to the sea. The sky was like a water colour painting streaked with pinks and oranges. It is one of the most amazing sights I have ever seen.

The flight home wasn't so great. I was exhausted and had picked up a throat infection. I was so tired I could barely keep my eyes open. As we descended I could feel the pressure building in my head. It didn't feel like this going to Ibiza?? The pain in my ears was unbearable and I covered them with my hands and winced. My ear drums burst touching down in Liverpool, and then I completely lost my voice for a week. The kids were thrilled! I had an amazing time in Ibiza and I couldn't wait to go abroad again.

The next year of my life was relatively normal and I was extremely contented. Jim and I ate breakfast in the garden together if it was sunny. We had barbeques and karaoke, garden parties for all our June birthdays, and I took the children on holiday in September to, *Hafn y Mor* in Wales. Here we visited castles and had cream teas. I learned to fence and even gave the instructor a run for his money. We skated at the roller disco and flew down the flumes at the on site pool. I had had my holiday in Ibiza so it was only fair for us all to go on a family holiday too.

I was very happy with Jim. We laughed ourselves stupid sometimes at each other. Nobody else would have found us remotely funny but we just had that same sense of humour. Always at ease in each others company. We were like brother and sister.

He was my rock through everything I had been through. The nuisance neighbours and the problems with my family. The times when I believed that there was something wrong with me because of my Mum's rejections and criticism's, he'd reassured me.

With regards to my family I had always questioned myself, had I said the right thing? or, should I have said anything at all? Was it me that caused all the problems? I would go over the rows for days in my head trying to convince myself I had done nothing wrong.

I valued his opinion on the subject as he was on the outside looking in. To him the picture would be clearer. I always asked him to be honest with me and tell me if it was me in the wrong. I had tried so hard to make things work with my family. I had learned to kerb my temper and to compromise or negotiate with my Mum. I always tried to do the right thing and still these lapses of not speaking and the bitterness. I started to need answers about my life. Where had I been fostered and who was I with. I did ask my Mum at some point who had fostered me but her answer was "ooohhh I don't know." There were little gaps that needed filling in. That is when I wrote to Social Services requesting my file from care. There had to be a reason for this constant battle with my family. It took a few weeks whilst the information was gathered and I was invited to a day centre to view it.

A social worker sat with me when I received my file as did Jim….my rock. Two great big brown envelopes were brought to me containing, *my life*. I sat down and read through a lot of it straight away. There was too much to read all of it at once. There were little yellow labels to mark the most distressing parts. Some things I already knew, some had been dormant memories, others were shocking revelations. It was no wonder I had been the way I was as a child. Reading through it confirmed to me what I needed to know. I was not at fault for what had happened to me. However, I realised that it was no one else's fault for the things that happened in the past either. Mum had an illness that wasn't going to go away. I will never be able to decipher whether she plays on that illness sometimes or not. Maybe her manipulative nature is part of the illness. I had to learn to accept that things were never going to change, and to accept my Mum as she is. I believe that in her illness she thought what she did was the right thing. I don't hold any grudges against her. I love my Mum dearly and I know that deep down she loves me too. I also believe that it is the future and what happens now that matters and not the past. My past has made me who I am today and I wouldn't change a single thing.

Mum wasn't happy at all when she learned I'd had my file. She threatened to take me to court saying it was illegal to have the information given to me, and why didn't I just leave it alone. It was my right and I just needed to know.

29. I Love You

April 2003 was to see my whole life turned upside down again. Big Shaun and I had always been really good friends and he visited us quite often. He had offered me a ride on the back of his motor bike a few months before but I had declined. He arrived again on a cold April afternoon on his motorbike and this time I couldn't resist his offer. When I hopped on the back and rode off with him that was the moment that I fell in love!!!

I had seen him glimpsing at me occasionally in the past and I had always had a feeling something was there between us. I remember the first time I had felt something. It was when we were talking on the doorstep of my old house years before and his eyes had momentarily flashed a beautiful green in the sunlight. He was beautiful. I never thought for a second any feelings were reciprocated and I truly was happy with Jim, so no more feelings were ever dwelled upon.

I had always felt overly concerned for Shaun, wanting to find him a nice girlfriend. I'd always said he should have been snapped up years ago. The last girlfriend he'd had, had hurt him deeply and I remember putting my arms around his neck outside his work place and wanting to comfort him when he was upset. When his mother had passed away some years before I'd wanted to comfort him then too but I'd thought it may have looked odd. I asked Jim to go and offer his sympathies out of concern for him.

We joked a lot together, him saying, "why cant I find a nice blonde babe who likes cars and bikes?"

I would always reply tongue in cheek, "sorry, I'm taken. You can't have me."

I had always avoided brushing past him or being too near him. He made me nervous. I had never ever questioned why or even thought about it till now. It was just automatic. Now I knew why. I had been avoiding falling for him.

I kept my feelings to myself that was until I realised he had feelings for me too. He had passed a comment one night that left me in no doubt of how he felt about me. I was totally blown away and utterly overwhelmed that someone like him could be interested in me that way. It turned out that part of the reason he had not spoken to Jim and I for several months after announcing our wedding, was because of the feelings he had for me. All of a sudden a whole bunch of feelings in me rose to the surface. Feelings I had been suppressing for a long time until now. It dawned on me that the needs I had chosen to ignore with Jim thinking that they were not important, actually were important. I couldn't ignore them anymore.

For the next six weeks I battled inwardly. I had already gone against my Christian beliefs so many times. I'd married Jim for life and had meant every word I'd said to him on our wedding day. Now I was torn in two. I would go off to see Shaun in the evenings, spending more and more time with him. I knew it was wrong but he was like a drug and I couldn't get enough of him.

I know it sounds stupid but I loved Jim with all of my heart and I couldn't bring myself to have a full blown affair with Shaun. I couldn't have lived with myself if I had. Just seeing him was bad enough. Jim and I were like soul mates and we had been so happy until now. I had one failed marriage behind me and for another to end was beyond contemplation. But the more I saw of Shaun the more I realised what was missing in my relationship with Jim. I felt like a fifteen year old school girl again. We went out for drives in his car to car modifying shops and to Chester on his motorbike. When ever I wrapped my arms around him on the back of the bike I fell deeper and deeper. It got to a point where Shaun told me he loved me. I was shocked and could not, would not say it back to him. That would change everything. I needed to work out what I was going to do as this situation was not fair on anyone. I had never envisaged being apart from Jim, but now I could not envisage being without Shaun either. If anyone ever asks is it possible to love two men at the same time then the answer is yes. In different ways of course.

Things came to a head when I had to go down south with Jim to a family wedding in June. I didn't want to go as I was leaving Shaun for a weekend but I knew I had to be with my husband and do the dutiful thing. The day before the wedding was my birthday. Jim had organised a cake for me at the hotel we were staying in and I ended up having a few celebratory drinks with my sister in law. I sneaked off to the bathroom to phone Shaun on my mobile. I was missing him. He'd said to me if I texted him that night he would ring me straight back. When he didn't ring me back and texted me *'good night,'* instead I was heartbroken and cried. That was when I realised I did love him and so I texted it to him,

'I love you.'

Of course he thought it was the drink talking. I phoned him the next day to tell him I had meant what I had said. I was right, it did change everything.

Jim knew something was wrong. I was acting strangely because I felt guilty and I picked faults with him to make myself feel better. I also brought up the problems we had encountered years before unable to just ignore them anymore. I had been so happy to be in a good relationship rather than a bad one that certain things hadn't mattered until now. I had thought that after we were married things would just rectify themselves but they never really had. Now Jim said he wanted to make it work but it was too late. I didn't want to rectify it any more. He was too much like my brother. And that was it. I'd hit the nail on the head. He <u>was</u> like my brother. Soul <u>mates</u>. Mates not lovers.

Back at home I couldn't wait to see Shaun again. I told him if Jim asked me what was wrong I was going to tell him as I couldn't live like this anymore. I knew what I would be giving up but I didn't want to miss out any more either. The last thing I wanted to do was hurt Jim. He was a good man and my rock. I needed to be honest with him and get things out in the open before temptation got the better of both Shaun and myself. So that's what I did.

I came in one night from being with Shaun and he asked me what was wrong. This was my cue. I told him I had feelings for someone else and he guessed immediately that it was Shaun. It was obvious as I'd always told Jim I was with him. He'd just trusted us. Naturally he hit the roof at first throwing the phone across the kitchen and punching the door. I left the house for a while for things to calm down. I couldn't stand seeing the hurt I'd caused him. I know Jim didn't deserve it. When I came back to face the music things were surprisingly calm and easy. We talked until three in the morning and even joked about it. I still wasn't sure where things were going to go from here. It was all still fresh.

The right thing to do would have been to finish my relationship with Shaun and make my marriage work. I wished I could have wanted that, but I didn't. I knew if I stayed with Jim I would never feel the same again and I would end up feeling full of resentment. I felt that life was for living and didn't want to wake up in ten years time full of regrets and bitterness for not taking a chance. Shaun had jumped on his bike and rode off thinking if he was no longer on the scene that Jim and I could work things out. He planned to leave for a life somewhere else not thinking for a second I was serious about being with him permanently. The thought of losing him tore me apart. A few days on when I had taken time to think, I made my decision and telephoned Shaun. I told him whether he stayed or he left that I could not go back. It was over between Jim and I.

One of the hardest things I have ever done in my life was to split up with Jim. I didn't want to lose him either. The last six years had been the happiest of my life and we had been through so much together. I was giving it all up along with his family whom I had grown to love. I knew that this decision would affect my children too as Jim had been the only father figure that they'd ever really had. I contacted their Dad thinking at least if he was on the scene again maybe it would cushion the blow a little for them. After all the children were old enough now to decide if they wanted to see their Dad or not. I just hoped he wouldn't let them down again this time round.

Jim and I remained friends through the whole thing. I even went house hunting with him to find his new place. The fact that it was all so amicable made me even surer I was doing the right thing. When he moved out in August 2003 we all cried at the door when we said our good byes. I will never forgive myself for the pain I put him through. I know I was selfish and it was my choice to be with Shaun, but I really did miss Jim for a long time afterwards and I went through a kind of grieving process.

I had always said that nothing could test my faith again after my Mum falling out with me the last time, but I was wrong. Why now after everything had been calm and my life was in order was temptation put my way. I blamed God for testing me. My trust in Him sorely lapsed now even though the situation was of my own doing. I stopped going to church. I felt like a hypocrite in God's house after what I had done. Nevertheless I had made my decision and it was final.

It wasn't easy at first. I felt guilty all the time and I was concerned for Jim. I felt responsible for making sure he was going to be alright given that he hadn't put himself in this position.... I had. He still came down and visited us which would appear to be a strange thing to most people, but I was glad that we stayed friends. His and my opinion was, what was the point of fighting about it? His acceptance of the situation just made me realise how much like brother and sister we had been. Sometimes we still had a laugh and other times I felt awkward around him. He would make uncomfortable comments and I was never really sure if it was his humorous side or if he was having a dig at me. I felt I deserved his sarcasm anyway and so I said nothing. The months passed by quickly.

In October 2003 Shaun, myself and the kids went on holiday to Majorca. I was glad to get away after the last few months of upheaval. I wanted to take the children abroad as I had never been myself until last year and this would be great for them. I remember feeling that Mediterranean heat as soon as we stepped of the plane. We stayed in a quaint little villa apartment in Cala d or. It was a wonderful holiday. The tiny emerald coves around the island were where we spent most of our days. The children played happily in the sand and on their lie lows in the shimmering sea. We bought fresh pineapples on the beach from one of the locals who cut it in experienced fashion in front of us. I have never tasted anything so mouth-watering. Away from the routine of school, cooking, washing, meetings and general daily life we could be free and just be.

I hired a car to take us for days out and drove on the other side of the roads which was an experience in itself. It was weird having the gear stick on the right and not the left side. The people there drove like bats out of hell!!

We visited the, *Caves of Drac,* and the *Caves of Ham,* said to be home to some of the largest underground lakes in the world. We were shown through by a local guide who continuously snorted phlegm from the back of his throat with no shame whatsoever. He took us deeper and deeper stumbling into the damp glistening caves whilst making the most grotesque noises ever. Shaun and I giggled. Stalagmites and stalactites surrounded the caves and we marvelled at the shapes and sizes of them. Deeper still in the heart of the caverns was a huge lake lit by dim lights. It was so clear you could see through it for miles. We were then shown to a seating area made slightly dodgy by the wet ground and damp atmosphere and we waited. Then from another part of the lake beyond part of the cavern came little boats that floated across the vast lakes and on board were orchestras playing their instruments. This truly was a magical event. When the concert had finished there were boats lined up to take us back on a different route for the way out. *Fascinating!*

We had a fantastic family night out at the, Son Amar. We went by coach to a five star hotel where a show took place whilst we dined around the stage. The meal was fabulous and the waiters could not do enough for us. There were bottles of orangeade for the kids and wine for the adults. After our starters of tapas, spit roasted chicken, chips and salad was then placed on the table for us to help our selves. Then later our desert arrived of ice-cream. The kids were really excited. The show began and was compiled of snippets from several different shows such as, Carmen, River dance and Chicago .there was a trapeze act in luminous suits which zipped over the audience on wires. To finish there were comic acts and lastly, The Drifters.

The holiday kind of cemented us all together as a family. Shaun was brilliant with the kids and took them on in a way I had never expected him to. Even when I was with Jim, I had always felt that the children were my responsibility and I had more or less managed them single handed. That was just the way it had been and it wasn't ever a problem. Now I had support and it was a strange thing. It just seemed to come natural to Shaun. I suppose it helped that the kids had known him for so long before we had got together too.

Soon it would be Christmas again. It would be strange this year without Jim. I tried to keep everything normal for the kids. I took my usual photos of them under the tree and Jim did come to see us on Christmas day. We exchanged gifts and the atmosphere wasn't too bad.

Then in January 2004 I received shock news.

My sister was pregnant...............with Jim's baby!

30. The Avon Lady!

I heard the news on the grapevine.

My initial reaction was, don't be soft, she can't have kids.

I wondered if it was just a vicious rumour to annoy me. I knew Jim had been going up to see her and they had got close, but I didn't think they were that close.

When I found out from Jim that she really was pregnant I was astounded, but I can honestly say hand on heart I was well made up for her and Jim. All this time believing she couldn't get pregnant and one night with my ex husband proved that she could. It must have been, *meant to be.* A part of me was envious. I wished the baby she was carrying was mine. Not because I wanted Jim back, but because I had always wanted another baby after what had happened with my last pregnancy. It was weird, my sister carrying a child to the man I was still married to.

Jim and I had discussed having a baby when we were together but I had always put it off saying, in five years and, "when the time is right." I had made the decision years ago to not have any more children until I knew the three children I already had were settled and happy. They had been through a lot in their young lives and so they came first. Every year that had passed I was still saying, in five years making the stretch grow longer. Obviously my reasons for putting it off and putting it off were subconsciously because something had never felt quite right between us.

I was genuinely pleased for Tracey. It did cross my mind that maybe sleeping with my ex husband was an act of revenge. After all she hadn't spoken to me now for two years. She didn't think she would get pregnant so why not? I went through an angry stage thinking why was Jim going up there to see her anyway? It's just not the done thing. She was my sister and he was my ex. Jim knew what I had been through with my family and I felt he had now betrayed me in retaliation for my betrayal to him.

My anger didn't last that long. I was too happy that I was going to be an aunty for the first time and I wasn't qualified to dish out the do's and don'ts anyhow after ending up with Shaun.

I know it is an unspoken rule that you don't date your sisters ex boyfriends or husbands. A friend of mine had said to me on the subject, "I would never speak to my sister again if she did that to me. You just don't go there with your sister's ex."

My conclusion of the situation after much thought was, why should I be angry with them? I had made the decision not to be with Jim so he could see who he liked. My sister had suffered emotionally through her life and she had also been affected by our childhood but in a different way to me. I think that she was lonely. She like me grasped any affection that came her way and I couldn't blame her for that. Jim was lonely too and my theory is that they found comfort in each other. How could I stand in the way of that? If they had found happiness together then I was genuinely happy for them and on the plus side Jim was still going to be part of my family now. I didn't have to lose him after all. The only problem I had now was that Tracey still wasn't speaking to me.

I had just finished modifying my beloved Peugeot 205 in August just gone so now I took on another challenge. In February I bought a fire blade 400 motor bike and I started taking bike lessons. I passed my theory test and my C.B.T. Now I just needed to pass my bike test. My car had been in the garage for eight weeks having a body kit fitted with a huge animal front bumper and St Tropez rear bumpers. I had huge side skirts that twisted in the middle and a smoothed, de-locked tailgate. I had the whole car colour coded and sprayed up. The finishing touches were a single aluminium wiper blade and silver foil graphics. It was amazing when it was eventually finished and a real head turner, especially when I blew flames out of the exhaust at the cruises we went to!! I was very proud and the kids loved going out in it. I dropped them off to school in the mornings and picked them up at home time as they loved showing off to their mates in it.

At Easter, eight months after my contacting their Dad, access became an issue again. I knew deep down it wouldn't have lasted long. Little Shane had been caught pinching one of his dads cigarettes and having a sly smoke. His dads reaction was to ban him from the house. Complete over reaction and plain cruelty in my eyes. I pleaded with him on the phone not to reject his son for one silly mistake. I mean, who hasn't had a sly fag at that age? Not many of us. By denying his son the right to go to his house to see them, I felt that this would only fuel anger and frustration in him creating a worse situation. Shane needed stability as did Coral and Michael. For years contact had been irregular and had never settled in to a proper routine. The Christmases and birthdays when contact was non existent were the worst thing, when they didn't receive so much as a card or a phone call from him. It wasn't fair to them.

In August 2004 I took on yet another challenge. My Avon area manager, Judy called to see me one day to congratulate me on how well I was doing with my sales. I had been doing very well with Avon for a few years now and I had become one of the top ten percent Avon representatives in the country. I had reached fifth place one particular year and third another year for my area's highest sales awards. Judy told me of a new exciting opportunity becoming an Avon sales leader. She said as I was a very able rep and that maybe I was capable of showing other people how to sell Avon too which is basically what it entailed. It sounded interesting but it was the summer holidays. I had three kids running me ragged so I wanted to wait till they were back at school and then look in to it. Nah not me, I plunged in at the deep end.

I became a self employed sales leader and quickly started appointing and managing new Avon representatives in to a team which I would then earn from. I went along to business meetings and learned a lot from Judy who also became a true and trusted friend. My book keeping skills now came in to force as I started keeping my own accounts and I became self employed. Something I had always dreamed of doing. I'd had other jobs in the past but nothing that had ever really suited me.

The Avon Lady!

Working in a local school as a dinner lady was one of them. Unfortunately it was at the time when I had become quite ill and so I had left after a few weeks as it was too much for me to cope with. I enjoyed it but I didn't want to kill myself doing it. I'd also been a lollypop lady for the grand total of only nine days. After nearly being ploughed down on several cold and frosty mornings by impatient and ignorant drivers I gave it up. Definitely not for me!! Our lollypop men and ladies our treasures to be proud of. They do a fantastic job for our school children with not nearly enough appreciation. At least I'd learned that. After all these years of searching for the right job I realised I had been doing it all along. Avon was what I was good at. Selling make up, smellies and gabbing to the neighbours, and now I was showing others how to do it too. Perfect!

In October the news reached me that my new baby nephew had been born. I had passed some gifts on through Jim a while back when she was pregnant and I hoped that one day my sister would know they were from me. I remember going to the shops and buying a fleecy blanket and some other cute baby things. I gave them to Jim and asked him to give them to her without mentioning they were from me. I didn't think she would except them if she knew. He didn't need to let on that he hadn't bought them and she would just assume he had. She ended up going through most of the pregnancy on her own as things were strained with her and Jim and they had split up. I felt really bad for her. No one should have to go through it alone. I'd wanted to be involved but she still refused to speak to me. I so wanted to see the baby and be there for Tracey but I didn't dare build my hopes up for fear of rejection again. Not only that, but it wasn't just us any more. I didn't want her baby to maybe get attached to me and then I disappear because of a non speaking situation. That wouldn't be fair.

In December 2004 when my nephew was eight weeks old my Mum finally contacted me to say that my sister wanted us to see him. I had always wanted to have my family around me and just forget about the past. I wanted my kids to have their Dad and Nan and auntie's. Just to be a normal family and not to fall out over pointless things. Now my opinion seemed to be shared. Tracey wanted her child to have his cousins and aunty. Funny how having children changes your out look on life. We spent a day together over Christmas. I met my baby nephew and I cuddled him affectionately not realising at the time, that against the odds, I too was now pregnant!!

I didn't believe it first. I'd had the coil for five years so I had thought my missed period was something to do with my thyroid condition. In January 2005 I did a pregnancy test just to rule it out. It showed positive, but it wasn't very clear so I asked Shaun to bring home another, different one from work.

I recall saying to him, "pick up one of those expensive blue ones, which will be clearer."

I nearly fell off the toilet seat when it showed up pregnant straight away. How could I be? I still had the coil fitted.

The strange thing was, I had been to the clinic earlier that week to have it removed as it was causing me a few problems. Shaun and I had discussed trying for a baby in the near future as we were settled now, so I had decided on taking the contraceptive pill instead for the time being. There was an hour long wait at the clinic so I'd ended up having to leave before I was seen as I had to get back for the children coming home from school.

My third test at the doctors confirmed my pregnancy and I cried with happiness. I was well chuffed!! Again I thought, this is definitely meant to be.

A few weeks in to my pregnancy I started to bleed and have abdominal pain. I was admitted to hospital on a Friday to await a scan. I worried that the coil was damaging my baby or I was going to miscarry because of it. I had to wait all weekend as the scan unit was not open until Monday. I had the scan two days later which showed the amniotic sack but the doctor said she couldn't see my baby. I craned my neck to look at the screen willing my infinitesimal life form to appear there and relieve us all. All I saw was the black dot the doctor had been referring to. I had drank lots of water before the scan and was desperate for the loo now. I couldn't go. I was petrified of letting go and the nerves had overtaken my body.

I shook like an autumn leaf and thought to myself, they're going to have to operate to extract my wee.

Another of several blood tests came back and they said they could not confirm that I was still pregnant. The hormones in my blood were not doubling up the way they should have been and this was worrying. Shaun and I were in bits.

It was decided that whether I was still pregnant or not my coil had to be removed. If I was still pregnant then it could cause a miscarriage anyway so I was more at risk leaving it where it was. Just as I made the decision to go ahead and have it removed the doctor came rushing in saying there had been a mistake with my blood tests and she had been looking at the wrong one. The latest test which she had now found confirmed I was definitely still pregnant. We cried with relief. Now all I had to do was hope that I didn't miscarry after my coil was removed.

I was kept in over night just in case and I swore to high heaven I would never have the coil fitted again.

The next day all my pain had completely vanished and I felt fine. It seems that my body had been trying to reject my coil and now that it was gone, my pregnancy could progress normally.

At my twenty week scan an abnormality was detected. My baby's kidneys were dilated and swollen which signified a blockage of some sort. It was thought to be a condition called, *renal valves*. Water was not passing out properly causing a back log of fluid in his kidneys and bladder, in turn causing them to swell. I had to go to the hospital for regular scans from then on. There was talk of delivering the baby early if need be or operating through me to release some of the fluid pressure from him.

In June At twenty nine weeks pregnant I had another appointment at the hospital. After being left in a hot sweaty room for forty minutes with no air conditioning, we were then told by a doctor that our baby probably had downs syndrome as renal valves were associated with it. She said I could consider other options available to me. I was horrified. I knew what the doctor was suggesting but I couldn't quite take it in.

The Avon Lady!

I asked her, "what do you mean; I'm twenty nine weeks pregnant?"

Her answer was, "well in your case we would make an exception."

"No way."

She was quite persistent and seemed to pressure me for an answer there and then. She asked would I like some information on downs syndrome if I was going to keep the baby, but I couldn't think straight. Of course I was going to keep my baby. I could feel him kicking inside me. I'd already named him and I chatted to him when I was in the bath. She waffled on a while longer to Shaun. Everything she said to us was like a distant murmur to me. My head was buzzing and the room was hot and stuffy. I had to get out of there. I got up and ran from the room, floods of tears blinding me. I just needed to go home and be with my family. It was my daughters fourteenth birthday that same day and I had organised a party for her for when we got back from the hospital. I had to get home for her. I had to put on a brave face, light the candles on Corals birthday cake and try to put things to the back of my mind. I greeted the guests and sat in the garden whilst Coral opened her presents. She was blissfully unaware, as was everyone else.

I was a blur for a few days after that and sunk in to a depression. I could feel my baby somersaulting inside me and moving about. I had already named him and loved him. He was part of me and Shaun. How could the doctor have suggested I terminate him at this late stage. If he did have downs we would cross that bridge when we came to it. He would still be our baby no matter what. I couldn't rest.

I eventually telephoned the hospital and told them what had happened at my appointment and I was put on to the specialist doctor. The doctor put my mind at ease after days of worry by telling me it was <u>not</u> likely that our baby had downs syndrome and we shouldn't have been told that. Although renal valves can be associated with downs syndrome, it was more likely <u>not</u> the case, in our case. He explained that our baby probably had a little blockage so that when he had a wee it was rather like pushing against a door. So much water was passing through it but then the door swings back the other way causing, *reflux,* or fluid to go back up the wrong way, thus swelling his kidneys. Now that made sense to me!!

The doctor we had seen on our last visit had been somewhat insensitive in her explanation. I felt relieved after this latest explanation, not totally but enough to carry on with hope.

The remainder of my pregnancy was fraught with teenage shenanigans.

On the fifteenth September 2005 I went in to labour.

31. Mysterious Life

Shaun rang work and told them he wouldn't be coming in that day. I stayed in bed all day listening to, Chicago and, phantom of the opera amidst my contractions. It relaxed me. Eventually when the pain began to get too much I knew it was time to go to the hospital. At one point I thought I was going to give birth in the car. Every bump in the road seemed to bring the contractions on stronger and I winced. We parked up at the hospital and I hobbled my way across the car park in my slippers in the rain. What a dozy mare!!! You'd think by my fourth child I may have known to phone the hospital and let them know we were on our way. I may have known that Shaun could have dropped me right outside the maternity units' doors. Somehow I managed to miss that so they weren't prepared for my arrival.

After being admitted I found that rocking side to side was easing my pain....that was until the nurse came in and told me I needed to be dripped up for a caesarean and I had to lie on the bed. This was a precaution as I'd had an emergency section with Michael. I was gutted!!

I was only in labour for about two hours. The nurse came in and told me at this stage if the baby wasn't going to make an appearance soon then it would be down to theatre for me. With that I tried a little push and that was it. He was coming. I turned my head away from Shaun and I groaned like a cow. I squeezed his hand with all my strength and hoped to God I hadn't ruined my image!! Ewan (named after Ewan Macgregor) was born at 7pm on the dot.

As soon as he arrived we were delighted when he weed all over the nurse. At least his bladder was emptying. I breast fed him straight away after tucking his naked little body up my nighty and we bonded immediately. He had a scan and a blood test the next day and as his kidneys were still dilated he was transferred to Alder hey children's hospital. My poor baby was like a pin cushion. I was further away from home now and there was no way I was going to leave my baby and go back home, besides I wanted to breastfeed him. For the first three nights I stayed in a tiny room in the corridor so I was at hand. It was confirmed that he did have renal valves and he would need an operation.

At five days old he had an operation to remove the valves that were causing the blockage. He had to have a catheter fitted until his fluid ran clear. We sat in the waiting room until he was ready to go down to theatre. I felt so useless as he was wheeled away on his hospital bed. All we could do now was wait. I remember his little face weary with the anaesthetic when he came back up to the ward. So tiny but so strong!! Sadly one of his kidneys didn't recover from the damage and he only has one that functions normally. Doctors say it is possible for him to live a normal life thankfully. He takes regular medication and he has check ups and scans every few months.

I wish I had taken to motherhood years ago the way that I have now. It is the most fun, fulfilling and wonderful thing I have ever done. My life was now filled with baby bounce and rhyme at the library and booby (breastfeeding) clinic sessions. With one baby I could take note of every milestone. I couldn't do that before when I had three children and things were so hectic. Every moment with him is precious. Life is precious. I suppose age and maturity are a factor and having a good partner also definitely helps.

Heartache was to come for me later on in the New Year. I was taking my baby to clinic one day in February 2006 when I received some devastating news. I remember the day as clear as a bell. Even the spot where I was stood at the time. I am not going to divulge what that news was as it is too recent and still too painful. Its also not just my story but someone else's story too. All I can say is, is that it rocked me to the core.

It had snowed the night before and the ground had a thin sheet of snow settling on it. It was still snowing now. My baby was cuddled up in his big blue and white checked pram as I walked up the road. My mobile phone rang in my pocket and I answered. I listened to the lady speak as the spiky flakes of snow drifted into my hair and eyes. My frozen angry hands gripped my phone like I could shatter it into tiny pieces. From that moment everything turned upside down. Everything that I had ever done to keep my family together just ripped apart at the seams. I went straight into the clinic and broke down to my health visitor. I had already failed the test they give you after giving birth. I'd had a low score meaning that I had been on the verge of depression anyway. The health visitor had been keeping close contact with me but now this was the icing on the cake for me.

I have never ever been as depressed as I became now. I barely went out the door not able to face the world. Everything was a chore. I had nightmares and weird thoughts. I wanted to die!! I kept imagining things like walking in front of a bus or slipping into the road. That would be quick and hopefully not too painful. My mind warped with various other accidents like my head coming off like the scene in the film, *the omen*. I thought "I've failed my kids now anyway." They would be fine without me. Pete would have to take his children now. He would have no choice and Shaun would be a brilliant Dad to Ewan. But Ewan was so little and he needed me. I was breast feeding him .No one else could do that. He was the one thing that kept me going.

I was referred to the doctor and began a course of anti depressants. I was also referred to a local family group for support. I went along one Monday morning to the local church hall where the sessions are held and I was welcomed with open arms. I immediately felt supported and people understood what I was going through. The people there were all so lovely. The situation I was in wasn't going to go away but here I found firm friends and comfort when I needed it.

I had been to this church hall before to a Mums and tots session. I went for a few weeks but had stopped going as I had felt uncomfortable - like I didn't fit in. This must have been due to my state of mind. Now that I was at the family group I thought I would give it another try. I still go now….and gradually I have come back to my faith.

I look back now and I wonder how I managed with three children on my own, with no job, relationships gone wrong and some big old messes. I have made mistakes and I've done my damnedest to correct them. I'm not perfect and I never will be, but God loves a trier!!! It is only now that I realise through all my doubts and the times my trust in God has waned that he has always been there... by my side. *That's how I managed!!*

Through my catalogue of disasters and the many things I have done wrong, I know that there is a place in heaven for me.

There is a reason for every event that takes place in our lives. Sometimes we don't see what those reasons are at the time. Sometimes our prayers don't get answered immediately and sometimes the answers we do get are not what we expected, but they do get answered.

I believe that all our children are part of Gods plan and that; He definitely does work in mysterious ways.

32. Somewhere

I had looked for my Dad on many occasions since he'd left his bulldozed flat. I'd had an address for him which I'd been given after I had received my Social Services file several years ago. I didn't hold out much hope of him being there after all that time but I had to find out. I knew he had gone to London at some stage. Had he even come back? I didn't know. I had psyched myself up for a reunion just in case and headed down to Birkenhead. I pulled up in the road I had been given. On the left hand side of the tiny side street I ended up in, was a small housing estate and on the right was a huge great red brick wall. Like the back of a factory or something. The houses to my left all had their own street names and the number I had for my Dad should have been where the great wall was. There were only two doors in the middle of the factory wall but neither had numbers on. I did knock on them to ask for information but I got no answer. It didn't add up.

I knocked on a few houses on the estate and asked residents if they knew where this number was on the tiny side street. No-one had a clue. I eventually resigned myself to the fact that the address must not have existed. I eventually jumped in my car to leave which promptly broke down in the street. I was stuck there for half an hour waiting for Jim to come and rescue me. I just wanted to get out of the road. Sitting there was torture…just another

Somewhere

dead end and the reality that I may never find my Dad. I did come back here several times out of curiosity and drove out of the end of the street and over the main road to see if the road extended further, but no. It was just more factories. Mum told me Dad was probably in a building somewhere near by watching all the idiots standing there trying to fathom it out. She said he was a bit of a joker and it was more than likely a fake address.

The next time I decided to look for Dad was when Shaun and I had planned to get married. Dads are supposed to give their daughters away so it had prompted me to look for him again. I thought he would probably still be here, in Birkenhead but how to find him? I had been around all the pubs in Birkenhead asking if anyone knew him. I didn't picture him as a drinker but it was somewhere to start. I may get lucky. I always wondered, would he be looking for me, does he think about me and my sister, would I have any half brothers or sisters?" Nobody knew him in the pubs. I have forgotten who it was I rang to find out which doctors surgery he may be registered with. I had guessed at a surgery which was the nearest one to his previous address and suggested this to the lady on the end of the line. The lady couldn't give me any information due to the data protection act. I explained to her that I was looking for my Dad and hadn't seen him for over twenty years now. She must have felt a twang of pity and told me, "all I can say is, is that your information is correct." That way she hadn't actually told me but I knew then that the surgery I had <u>was</u> where he was registered I left a letter at the surgery along with a photo of the children but it came to nothing. I also subscribed to genes reunited and started to build my family tree. My Dads name didn't come up so I had reached yet another dead end.

I got married on May 12th 2007 at Wallasey town hall. I had to go into this marriage with the view I would take each day as it comes. As a Christian I have already gone against my beliefs so many times. This time I have to make it work. I really wanted to be married again. I know its sounds silly but I had been content in my last marriage even though it eventually went wrong. I wanted that contentment again with Shaun. We hadn't gone through what we had gone through to not spend the rest of our lives together. I felt guilty about getting married for a third time and battled once again with my conscience about what was the correct thing to do. What would I wear? Would I look stupid? I had to remember that this was Shaun's first marriage and his day too. It would be unfair to deny him what he wanted for his big day.

I opted for a very pale pink and silver colour scheme. In fairness the colour scheme is a woman thing so he left that to me. My dress was not over the top which would be fitting for a third marriage but beautiful enough to make my new husband proud of me. It was cream and strapless with a delicate spattering of crystals on the bodice part. The back of the bodice was a very on trend lace up style. It was perfect.

I sat the night before drinking champagne and strawberries with my bridesmaids….my next door neighbour and my baby's god mother. My daughter was supposed to be a bridesmaid also but for reasons of her own she decided not to come to the wedding. Her dress hung waiting for her just in case she changed her mind.

I was hurt that she didn't turn up but I was not going to let it spoil the day. The dresses were silver satin and both bridesmaids looked stunning. Ewan (20 months old now) had the cutest little suit with waistcoat and cravat.

I had sent out for bacon butty's on the morning of the wedding to ease the panic and then went to have my hair done at a local hairdresser. The young girl was expert and quickly pinned my hair up and fitted my tiara. Back at home the flowers arrived…pale pink roses with diamantes set between them. Everything was running smoothly, even when Ewan picked up a bottle of nail varnish remover and tipped it all over himself soaking his suit. My poor bridesmaid was mortified. She had left the lid off not thinking. Well you don't when you haven't got children of your own do you? My instincts kicked in instead of panicking. I just peeled the jacket of him, doused it in cold water and then dried it with my hairdryer. It's one of those classic moments which you never forget on your big day.

I arrived at the town hall but I couldn't see anyone I knew waiting outside. Where was everyone? Where was Shaun? I was confused. I was then greeted inside by a lady who told me Shaun had arranged for everyone to be seated inside. Aha!!! Panic over I climbed the stairs lifting my dress so I didn't trip up on the skirt. I arrived at the doors and entered the room to Justin Timberlake's, *My Love,* playing in the background. Shaun couldn't have chosen a better song.

I scanned around the sea of faces and noticed my sister and my Mum both missing. They hadn't been speaking to me again for the last year or so. Who knows why this time. I can't even remember but I had bumped into Tracey a few weeks prior to the wedding and I had invited them both. They had also both confirmed they would be here so I expected them. If they hadn't said they were coming then it wouldn't have bothered me so much but to confirm and then not show up was devastating. I walked down the aisle and tried to push it to the back of my mind. That wasn't the most important thing today and I would deal with it later. Then I saw Shaun waiting for me and I melted.

It was in September 2008 I received an email. The email was from genes reunited telling me there was a match for my Dad in another family tree. I didn't get too excited. I received emails quite often that came to nothing although I hadn't had any in a while. I clicked the link to take me to the site and check it out anyway. The tree owners name just happened to be the same name as one of my dads brother's... my uncle. I had never ever met my uncle and I pondered whether this was just a coincidence. I emailed him asking about my Dad and was he possibly my uncle. After all it could all just be a mistake. I received an email back asking me what my sister's name was. This was obviously to clarify who I was. Only I would know her name proving I was who I said I was. I responded and in turn his family tree was opened up for me to view. At the same time I received another email from a random lady. I don't know who she was or how she knew who I was looking for but she mailed me with my uncle's name, his wife's name, their address and a telephone number. This was too good to be true. I didn't need to think twice picking up the phone immediately. My fingers trembled with anticipation. I didn't even know if they would want to speak to me or if he would know where my Dad was anymore. I dialled the number and after a few rings a man answered the phone. I was so nervous instead of asking for my uncle I asked for his wife. I don't know why. I explained who I was and that I had received his details in an email. I hoped he didn't mind me ringing him out of the blue. The man confirmed he was my uncle. At last family! We chatted for around half an hour. I couldn't believe it. I then moved on to the subject of my Dad telling my uncle I had been looking for him for twenty two years now. My uncle also had not seen my Dad for the same length of time as me as unfortunately they had had a falling out many years ago. My face fell. Another hope gone, although I was so happy to have found an uncle. He then proceeded to tell me the last address he'd had for my Dad. I was stunned when he relayed to me the same address I'd had. The same address I'd looked for nine years before. The fake address!

I said, "No, no I've been there. It doesn't exist."

My uncle replied, "of course it does."

"No, there's nothing there. Just a factory wall."

"Yes that's right," my uncle said knowingly.

"But I went there and it was just two doors in a wall, there's no flat there."

My uncle then said, "There is a flat there. I know because I stayed with him years ago."

I was confused. How could I have missed it? I needed to go back now and check again, just for my sanity.

It was Monday 29th September. My friend had just

had a baby and I had arranged to go and see her today. I dropped my little one off at his school at half past twelve so I had a few hours to spare. I jumped in the car and set off for her house as planned. When I got there my friend wasn't in. I sat for a moment. She must have forgotten about it.

Mmmmm, what can I do now?

I turned the car around and decided to go back down to Birkenhead. Spur of the moment decision. I may as well check it out once and for all. I knew he probably wouldn't be there now. Not after all this time. I drove to the place I had been once before. I turned in to the little road once again. At first I noticed the houses that had been on the left were gone. Now there was just an empty neglected space strewn with weeds and grass. Then I noticed a single car parked in the road. Just one car all on its own. My whole body surged with a nervous electric current. I was on pins. I just knew instantaneously. That would be my Dads car. I just knew it. I parked behind it and got out. There were the same two doors in the middle of the wall, only now one door had a huge great number nine on it and an intercom button. I pressed the button anxiously.

A muffled voice came over the intercom.

"Hello, who is it?"

"Hello, hello." I said straining to be heard properly through the crackles.

"Hello," I repeated.

The door buzzed open and the voice shouted down the stair well again,

"Who is it?"

I looked up toward the voice of the man standing peering over the balcony.

"Dad, it's me."

The man now almost speechless thought I was from the council (bless him) and said again.

"Who?"

I turned to mount the stairs.

"Let me have a look at you."

And there he stood. My Dad. Twenty two years of searching now over. The same face with smiley eyes but now with grey wispy hair and his moustache gone. He gripped the handrail to steady himself.

"Dad it's me, Gina."

I threw my arm around his neck. He still wasn't sure and gripped my arm pushing me back to look at me... checking it was definitely me. The reality dawned and he ushered me into the flat.

My search was over. I couldn't believe he had been here all this time. I had knocked on this very door nine years ago. Maybe I just wasn't meant to find my Dad back then. Maybe things wouldn't have worked out the way they have now. I don't regret not knocking back here earlier, as all those years ago I had a different life with different problems. Life is too short for regrets and as I said earlier everything happens for a reason. God has a plan for us. All I can say is, if I had found Dad then things could have had a very different outcome.

My Dad is the most affectionate, selfless father I could have wished for. I know I have missed out, but then so does he. We have a fantastic relationship and are very close now and that's what counts. He is also reunited with his brother and family who we see often. I hold no grudges about the past. I don't need to hold grudges. Anger and bitterness just eat you up and absorb you. My Mum and my Dad were young back then. I was young when I had my children. Kids don't come with an instruction leaflet. We all have problems and we all make mistakes. The good news is I am forgiven for my mistakes. My slate is washed clean with God. I know that he has lead me to where I am now(somewhere) and I couldn't have made it here without him.

I was lost, but now am found. *Luke 15:24*

Lightning Source UK Ltd.
Milton Keynes UK
12 January 2011
PP112560000 1B/1/P